Moses

The Man, The Messenger, The Mentor

By Dr. Dwayne C. Perry

Cover Design/Editor: NJ Kingdom Enterprises
www.njkingdomenterprises.com

Dedicated to all who have ever felt unqualified to lead or feared their message would go unheard. May this book inspire you to trust your journey and share your truth with confidence and boldness.

Acknowledgment

My deepest appreciation goes to everyone who has played a role in my journey from apprehension to assurance, as I discovered my voice and purpose as a messenger. The creation of this book, "Moses: The Man, The Messenger, The Mentor," has been shaped by the unwavering support, encouragement, and guidance of remarkable individuals who believed in my message even when I doubted myself. Thank you to my family, friends, mentors, and every reader who is striving to overcome fear and embrace their calling. Together, may we inspire one another to rise, speak truth, and lead with courage, as Moses did.

With gratitude,

Dr. Dwayne C. Perry

Table of Contents

Introduction

In journeying through the storied pages of biblical history, few figures captivate the imagination and stir the spirit as profoundly as Moses. In the narrative of his life, recorded vividly in the New King James Version (NKJV) of the Holy Scriptures, we encounter a man who was not only a prophet but also a leader, lawgiver, and mentor. Moses was a servant of God whose life continues to offer deep insights. Indeed, like none other, Moses is the modern-day model of leadership.

On a personal level, I connect deeply with Moses, as he is one of my 'Biblical Avatars.' As defined by Dr. Dharius Daniels, *"A Biblical Avatar is a scriptural figure whose life, mission, and calling align with a specific God-given assignment or purpose. These avatars serve as models or blueprints for modern-day believers who may struggle to see themselves reflected in contemporary society but can find their identity, mission, and divine calling through scripture."* As I study Moses, I see Me.

At the mention of his name, many of us recall Moses's encounter with the divine at the burning bush (Exodus 3:1-12). It is a powerful testament to how God calls

1

His people into a life of purpose and transformation. It is in that moment of revelation that Moses's timid nature was reshaped by the overwhelming call and authority of God, reminding us that true leadership is often birthed in moments of divine encounter. As a follower of Jesus, I have found that Moses's journey resonates deeply with the Christian walk, where revelation, obedience, and faith underpin our call to serve and lead.

By exploring Moses's life from his early years as a fugitive to his exalted role as a mediator between God and Israel, this book seeks to uncover timeless principles of leadership that continue to shape our understanding of authority, responsibility, and guidance. By reflecting on the NKJV scriptures, we see that Moses not only communicated God's laws but also modeled integrity, resilience, and servant leadership. His narrative challenges modern leaders to foster environments grounded in divine truth, accountability, and compassion.

Moreover, the lessons drawn from Moses's life are particularly relevant in the context of our journey in Christ. Just as his encounters with the Almighty transformed Moses, so too are we invited to be transformed by the revelation found in Jesus Christ. His teachings compel us to lead not out of self-interest, but out of a profound commitment to truth and justice, echoing the role of Moses as a lawgiver and visionary. In embracing both the regulatory and relational dimensions of leadership, Moses provides a paradigm that bridges ancient wisdom with contemporary calls to ministry and public service.

As we delve into the narrative of Moses, we will explore the interplay of divine revelation and human responsibility, a dynamic that continues to illuminate the path of effective and principled leadership. This exploration is designed not only to enrich our understanding of a seminal biblical figure but also to inspire us to lead lives marked by humility, boldness, and unwavering faith in the transformative power of God.

Part One exposes "Moses, the Man." His journey as a prophet begins with a divine encounter that transforms a reluctant man into a leader who channels God's will for His people. This section explores that pivotal moment as recorded in the New King James Version (NKJV) of Scripture, revealing both the grandeur of divine revelation and the practical lessons that resonate with believers today. From tending to sheep to leading a nation, the vulnerability, weaknesses, and strengths of the Man are so worth exploring.

In Part Two, "Moses the Messenger," we explore our own journey alongside Moses as God's messengers and mediators. Together, we will see how we are called to receive and communicate divine instructions, much like Moses did, and how we are entrusted to guide others through life's challenges. This section encourages us to reflect on what it means to bridge the gap between God and people, emphasizing our shared calling to spiritual leadership. Through Moses's example of obedience and resilience, we will uncover lessons that inspire our collective commitment to faithfully respond to God's call, lead with courage, and uphold the responsibilities placed upon us as His people.

Finally, in Part Three, "Moses the Mentor," we will discover how Moses invested in the lives of others by sharing wisdom, empowering future leaders, and nurturing faith within the community. Through his example, we learn valuable principles about equipping others, fostering spiritual growth, and leaving a legacy rooted in faithfulness and servant leadership.

Part
ONE
The Man

Chapter 1- The Reluctant Man

Before God's dramatic intervention, Moses lived a life marked by ordinary responsibilities and personal insecurities. Raised in the oppressive environment of Egypt, then growing up as a fugitive in Midian, Moses struggled with the weight of his identity and the possibilities of his future. His early years paint a picture of a man burdened by doubt, a man who questioned his worthiness to challenge the mighty Pharaoh and lead an entire nation out of bondage. It was a tall order, to say the least.

This reluctance is vividly portrayed in Exodus 3:11 (NKJV), where Moses asks, "Who am I that I should go to Pharaoh, and that I should bring the children of Israel out of Egypt?" His question reflects not only a fear of failure but also a deep-seated insecurity about his qualifications. Moses's initial perception of himself as inadequate is a powerful testament to the human tendency to doubt one's potential in light of seemingly insurmountable challenges. It is something we have all done.

Moses's turning point came during an ordinary moment of tending his father-in-law's flock on the rugged slopes of Mount Horeb. In Exodus 3:2 (NKJV), he encounters an extraordinary sight – a bush aflame yet not consumed by the fire. This mysterious phenomenon was no mere accident of nature; it was a carefully orchestrated moment of divine revelation.

At the burning bush, Moses is greeted by the unmistakable presence of God. The voice that emerges from the flames calls him "Moses" and declares a mission of epic proportions: to deliver the children of Israel from the tyranny of Egypt. In this encounter, God not only reveals His identity but also reassures Moses of His constant presence. Exodus 3:12 (NKJV) records God saying, "I will certainly be with you." This promise of divine accompaniment transforms Moses's perspective. Where he initially saw only his inadequacies, he now recognized that his strength comes from a power far greater than his own.

The burning bush is rich in symbolism. Fire purifies, transforms, and illuminates. Likewise, Moses's encounter served as a spiritual ignition, transforming his inner doubts into a resolute determination to fulfill God's will. As a follower of Jesus, I see a parallel in the transformative power of encountering Christ. Just as believers are called out of complacency into a life of purpose through Christ's revelation, Moses was propelled from his insignificance into a role of monumental significance. He is now postured to move from Reluctant to Ready!

Chapter 2- The Transformed Man

Following the burning bush encounter, Moses was confronted with a task that seemed overwhelmingly impossible: leading an enslaved people to freedom. The narrative of his life teaches us that divine strength often emerges in human weakness. Moses's initial protests, recorded throughout Exodus 4 (NKJV), reveal a man oscillating between reluctance and obedience. He expressed concerns about his speaking abilities, questioning, "What is that in my hand?" (Exodus 4:2, NKJV), and doubting his capacity to confront Pharaoh. Here, we see a Man in need of transformation!

The transformation from reluctance to resolve was not immediate but a gradual process marked by God's patient guidance. This gradual molding of character is a recurring theme in Scripture and resonates deeply with anyone who has experienced God's life-changing work. In my own spiritual journey as a follower of Jesus, there have been numerous moments when what seemed like my greatest limitation was, in reality, the arena in which God's power was most evident.

Moses's gradual acceptance illuminates the truth that the process of transformation often involves wrestling with doubt. In the face of repeated reminders of divine presence and provision, Moses moved from clinging to his self-doubt to embracing a larger destiny. His obedience, punctuated by small yet significant acts of faith, set the foundation for his extraordinary ministry. The fact that Moses was not an instantly transformed hero but rather a man who had to grow into his calling offers encouragement to all who feel unworthy or ill-equipped.

Central to Moses's transformation was the profound sense of divine assurance that accompanied every step of his mission. God's promise to be with him was not a generic blessing; it was a specific commitment that redefined Moses's identity and mission. In Exodus 3:12 (NKJV), the assurance "I will certainly be with you" is a mantra that echoes throughout the entirety of Moses's ministry. This phrase is a profound reminder that God's strength is made perfect in our weakness, and it calls every believer to step forward despite their limitations.

For Moses, the assurance of God's presence is what transformed him. It instilled in him the courage to confront Pharaoh, to challenge deeply entrenched social and political systems, and ultimately to lead a nation toward liberation. His journey was fraught with obstacles, yet it was marked by triumphs that were only possible because he trusted in the divine support promised to him.

For me, as a believer, this assurance brings deep comfort. In times of personal weakness, when life's challenges seem insurmountable, I am reminded that the same God who spoke to Moses is with me. The transformation of Moses validates that divine purpose transcends human frailty. It is not through our own strength, but through God's relentless commitment, that we are enabled to overcome our obstacles and fulfill our destinies.

True transformation comes with evidence. That evidence often manifests as character traits that were already there, just waiting to be unearthed. In Moses's case, those traits include Perseverance and Decision-Making. Let's explore them both.

Perseverance for Moses means more than simply maintaining his position; it involves the steady cultivation of hope even when the immediate circumstances seem bleak. His determination to lead despite myriad failures, whether navigating harsh terrains, dealing with conspiracies, or handling crises like the incident of the golden calf (Exodus 32), undercuts the superficial image of leadership as mere charisma or brilliant strategy. Instead, it highlights that resilience, rooted in faith and an unwavering focus on the long-term vision, is what truly defines great leadership.

In today's fast-paced world, challenges seem to manifest on multiple fronts, whether in career, personal relationships, or societal issues. Moses's perseverance offers a timeless reminder: perseverance is forged in the fire of adversity. When faced with setbacks, a leader who holds onto the vision and trusts in the higher purpose behind the struggle will inevitably gain not just external success but inner strength and wisdom.

For many, the journey towards any significant achievement is replete with hurdles. The story of Moses provides comfort by revealing that even the greatest leaders had moments of weakness and doubt. His continued resilience in leading a doubting and frequently rebellious people shows that perseverance does not always require a flawless exterior; it requires the humility to seek divine (or inner) strength and the courage to stand by one's commitment until the very end.

The NKJV emphasizes moments when Moses, despite personal and communal challenges, turned to prayer and dialogue with God. In moments when the people's discontent could have easily overwhelmed him, Moses stayed a mediator interceding for his people and reaffirming God's covenant promises (Exodus 32:11-14). His perseverance was not solitary; it was closely tied to his role as a bridge between God and His people. 13elation hints at a profound lesson: leaders who persevere often do so by seeking wisdom and grounding their decisions in a higher truth.

To continue, a critical aspect of Moses's effective leadership was his strategic approach to decision-making. Whether confronting Pharaoh, managing crises among the people, or responding to unexpected events, Moses was known for his thoughtful planning and consultation with God. His encounters with Pharaoh in Exodus illustrate how he strategically negotiated the release of the Israelites. Each act from the first inspection of Pharaoh's court to the subsequent plagues was a calculated move aimed at demonstrating the superiority of God's power over the earthly rulers. Moses's decisions were rooted in prayer, consultation, and an unwavering reliance on divine guidance.

Strategic decision-making is also evident during complex moments such as the splitting of the Red Sea (Exodus 14). Here, faced with the advancing Egyptian army and the seeming impossibility of escape, Moses followed God's command. The miraculous crossing was not just an act of divine intervention; it was the result of Moses's clear-headed strategic decision to trust in God despite overwhelming odds. His ability to remain calm and decisive, even in the face of imminent danger, highlights the importance of strategic thinking that balances faith with practical action.

Throughout the journey in the wilderness, Moses frequently had to make decisions that affected both the short-term welfare of the people and the long-term fulfillment of the divine promise. In Numbers, the episode of the twelve spies (Numbers 13-14) reveals the tension between immediate fears and the overarching promise of the Promised Land. When the majority of the spies returned with discouraging reports, the community's confidence faltered, endangering the fulfillment of the long-term vision. Moses, however, sought to reframe the perspective by reminding the people of God's past miracles and promises. Although his approach was met with resistance and a crisis of faith among the Israelites, his strategic emphasis on the future rather than the present laid an essential groundwork for eventual restoration.

For modern readers, this aspect of Moses's leadership underlines the importance of making decisions that do not sacrifice the long-term vision for immediate gratification or relief. Strategic decision-making involves juggling practical concerns with visionary goals. Leaders in every field must often decide between short-term fixes and actions that build toward sustainable progress. Moses's life teaches us that while immediate challenges must be addressed, they should not derail the pursuit of a larger, transformational purpose.

Another strategic element in Moses's decision-making was his willingness to seek counsel and delegate responsibilities. In Exodus 18, Moses's father-in-law, Jethro, observed that Moses was overwhelmed by the burden of daily leadership. Jethro advised him to appoint capable men as leaders over groups of thousands, hundreds, fifties, and tens, thus decentralizing judicial matters. By embracing this wise counsel, Moses demonstrated that effective leadership is not about doing everything alone but about empowering others and decentralizing authority. This not only reduced his personal strain but also built a more robust leadership structure within the Israelite community.

In today's context, strategic delegation is critical. Leaders must learn to trust their teams and establish systems of communication and accountability that ensure informed decisions at every level. Merlin-like discernment and strategic thinking, as seen in Moses's life, remind us that a leader's strength lies in the ability to identify and cultivate the potential of others, thereby extending the reach of the original vision.

The NKJV provides rich narratives in which Moses's strategic decisions are coupled with divine encouragement and pragmatic insights. For instance, when facing the imminent threat of the Egyptian army at the Red Sea (Exodus 14), Moses reassured the people with divine promises even as he prepared to act on God's command.

Such moments reveal that strategic decisions do not exist in a vacuum; they are intertwined with faith, prayer, and a deep-seated trust in a purpose that transcends the apparent realities.

Moreover, the dialogues between Moses and God (found throughout Exodus, Numbers, and Deuteronomy) illuminate the importance of pausing and seeking divine insight before taking action. Whether it involved choosing the right moment to confront Pharaoh or the wisdom to delegate authority as advised by Jethro, Moses's actions underscore the balanced interplay between prayerful contemplation and decisive action, a practice that continues to be relevant in situations requiring thoughtful risk management and rapid adaptation.

Strategic decision-making, too, is a lesson that resonates on a personal level. Whether it is choosing to delegate tasks, carefully weighing options, or pausing to pray (or reflect) before taking decisive action, Moses's approach provides a framework that is as applicable today as it was thousands of years ago. The balancing act between addressing urgent needs and nurturing a long-term vision is a universal challenge. Drawing inspiration from Moses, one learns that the key is to remain faithful to both

strategic planning and to the moment-by-moment decisions that move the vision forward.

In everyday leadership, whether in a workplace
team, a community project, or personal endeavors, the
idea that perseverance, coupled with strategic insight,
can overcome obstacles remains a timeless truth. Moses's
life reminds us that leadership is not defined solely by the
destination reached, but by the integrity, resilience, and
wisdom displayed along the way.

For contemporary leaders, Moses's example is
both an inspiration and a practical guide. Whether you
are tasked with leading a company through turbulent
times, inspiring social change, or simply guiding a family
through difficult decisions, the principles of vision, perseverance, and strategic decision-making are critical.
Moses teaches that when challenges seem insurmountable, let perseverance, fueled by faith and reflection, carry
you forward; and when decisions need to be made, draw
on both wisdom from experience and insight from those
you trust. In Moses's case, these traits were always present but activated only when he, the man, was transformed. So be it with us as well.

Chapter 3- The Vision of the Man

Central to Moses's leadership was his ability to cast a clear, compelling vision for the future. His mission to lead the Israelites out of Pharaoh's control was rooted in God's promise of land, freedom, and a future nation. This vision, articulated in God's commandments and promises, provided a concrete goal for the Israelites – a goal so powerful that it sustained them in the face of countless challenges along their journey. Moses's vision was not self-generated; it was divinely inspired. This distinction is crucial as it teaches modern leaders that an effective vision must be grounded in principles that extend beyond personal ambition. It must be God-Breathed!

Moses was renowned for his ability to communicate God's plan to a diverse and often skeptical people. By translating the abstract promise of deliverance into tangible steps such as confronting Pharaoh, performing miraculous signs, and guiding the people through the wilderness, Moses made the vision accessible. His leadership style was inclusive; he often held assemblies, listened to the concerns of his people, and sought divine confirmation before making critical decisions. For today's leaders, this highlights the importance of clear and consistent communication, ensuring that everyone understands and commits to the shared vision.

A key element in Moses's vision was his steadfast faith in God's promises, which allowed him to maintain trust even when the path was filled with uncertainty and setbacks. The promise in Exodus 3:12, "I will be with you," reassured Moses that the divine plan was attainable, regardless of the obstacles in his way. This unwavering trust served as a beacon for the Israelites, especially during times of crisis such as the perilous crossing of the Red Sea. Leaders today can take a lesson from Moses's trust: the ability to hold firm to a vision, even when facing daunting challenges, is essential for guiding teams and organizations through turbulent times.

Here is a key to vision that is often overlooked: Visionaries master humility. Moses's personal life was characterized by moments of vulnerability that endeared him to his followers. His willingness to confront his own doubts and shortcomings, as seen in his initial hesitation at the burning bush (Exodus 3:11), gave others the confidence to see him as authentic and relatable. Leaders who model humility and transparency foster a culture of honesty and mutual trust. Moses's eventual acceptance of his role, despite the self-doubt, serves as a powerful reminder that vulnerability is not a weakness but a strength, enabling leaders to connect more deeply with those they lead.

Other keys that mark the life of Moses, the Visionary, are Consistency and Integrity. Throughout his journey, he consistently adhered to God's commands, even when they defied conventional wisdom or personal comfort. His integrity was evident in his willingness to stand before Pharaoh, in the delivery of the Law at Mount Sinai, and in his persistence during the long wandering in the wilderness. These actions reinforced the trust his people had in him. For modern leaders, consistency and integrity are indispensable. Whether in business, politics, or community leadership, the commitment to a set of core values builds a reliable foundation for trust.

Another key that can't be overlooked is Empathy. Moses's leadership journey was not without personal struggles. His famous question, "Who am I that I should go to Pharaoh?" (Exodus 3:11, NKJV), underscores the deep-seated uncertainties he harbored about his own abilities. Yet, it is precisely through confronting and overcoming these doubts that Moses matured in his leadership. In dealing with personal obstacles, he developed a sense of empathy and understanding that was crucial for guiding a people as diverse and troubled as Israel. This evolution is particularly instructive for today's leaders, who often face imposter syndrome or self-doubt. Acknowledging personal limitations while actively seeking ways to overcome them can lead to a more robust and resilient leadership style.

In my own experience, embracing the lessons of Moses's leadership means acknowledging that vision often begins as a spark in times of personal adversity. It is in facing our own doubts that we discover the strength to articulate a purpose that is both meaningful and enduring. Whether in a community, a workplace, or a social initiative, trusting in that higher vision and communicating it transparently and compassionately can turn small efforts into movements with lasting impact.

Vision Casting: Seeing Beyond the Immediate

Moses's first encounter with a divine vision occurred when he beheld the burning bush (Exodus 3:1-6, NKJV). The bush, ablaze yet not consumed, was symbolic of God's eternal presence and the promise of renewal even amid trial. For Moses, this was the moment when an ordinary shepherd became the chosen instrument for a nation's deliverance. His vision was not of his own design but was divinely revealed as a call to move beyond immediate circumstances into a realm of liberation and hope.

This dramatic moment teaches us that true vision casting involves seeing the potential in a seemingly impossible scenario. The eternal flame of the burning bush became a metaphor for the destiny awaiting Israel. It was a destiny where suffering and bondage would give way to freedom, a new nation, and a closer relationship with God. Moses was given a future that eclipsed the harsh reality of slavery, and his role was to communicate this transcendent hope.

Once Moses was commissioned by God, his leadership journey became one of casting a grand vision for the Israelites. He was tasked with not only confronting

Egypt's severest oppressor, Pharaoh, but also speaking to a people demoralized by years of harsh slavery. Moses's dialogue with Pharaoh (Exodus 7-12) demonstrates his ability to articulate a vision of liberation. Through a series of signs and wonders, he was able to showcase that God's promise of deliverance was real and imminent.

In these encounters, Moses's vision was twofold: to convince those in power of God's authority and to inspire a subjugated people to believe in a future defined by hope rather than despair. His clear articulation of "I will bring you out" (Exodus 6:6-8, NKJV), even when doubts and resistance were palpable among the Israelites, stands as a testament to how a leader must focus on the end goal rather than the temporary setbacks. The vision was not only a distant promise but also a practical blueprint for action: leave Egypt, cross the Red Sea, enter the wilderness, and eventually inherit the Promised Land.

Modern leaders in all fields can draw from Moses's example of vision casting by understanding that great visions, whether they relate to social reform, corporate transformations, or community initiatives, are deeply rooted in a purpose larger than personal ambition. Moses's vision was grounded in God's promise, which gave him the authority and conviction to steer an entire nation. Likewise, leaders today benefit from aligning their vision with enduring values and long-term goals.

A visionary leader must communicate with clarity and consistency. Moses repeatedly reminded the Israelites of the Promised Land even when the journey seemed insurmountable. This long-term perspective is significant: even in the midst of great struggles, the vision remains a beacon that encourages perseverance and commitment. As a personal insight, when facing challenges in professional or personal realms, reflecting on the vision beyond immediate troubles can infuse the necessary determination to move forward.

Moses's journey did not merely consist of receiving a divine vision, it involved countless tests of character in the harsh wilderness. In the book of Numbers, for instance, the lack of immediate progress, the incident of the spies, and the constant murmurings of the Israelites put tremendous pressure on his leadership. Yet, Moses continuously relied on God's promises and revisited the earlier vision of liberation to spur forward the journey. It was the vision that kept him going!

Chapter 4- The Duality of the Man

The Interplay Between Humility and Authority

Moses's leadership is a study in contrasts. Duality is a common theme. Specifically, how to navigate the space between humility and authority. From the very beginning of his encounter with God, we see a man who is troubled by his own inadequacies. In Exodus 3:11 (NKJV), Moses asks, "Who am I that I should go to Pharaoh and bring the children of Israel out of Egypt?" This question is not simply a display of self-doubt; it is a profound declaration of humility. Moses did not see himself as inherently powerful. Yet, as the narrative unfolds, he assumes an authority that is both divinely granted and tempered by selflessness and compassion. Navigating this duality is a great skill!

Humility can be understood as the willingness to acknowledge one's limitations and to depend on God's guidance rather than on personal pride or ability. Moses exemplified this quality in several key passages: In

Exodus 3, after God reveals Himself through the burning bush, Moses remains overwhelmed and hesitant. His initial reluctance illustrates his awareness that he is not called for his own glory but to serve a far greater purpose. Later, when confronted with the enormity of the task facing Pharaoh and the might of the Egyptian empire, Moses continues to express his humble concern over his inadequacies (Exodus 4:10-13). His concern that he might not be eloquent enough, that he is "slow of speech and slow of tongue" (Exodus 4:10, NKJV), is not a sign of weakness but of a leader who is conscious of the gravity of his mission and the responsibility of conveying God's word accurately. This humility made Moses approachable and relatable to the people, who saw in him not a proud demagogue but a servant-leader, willing to fall on his knees before God. His humility is not self-deprecating but rather an acknowledgment that his authority comes not from his own merit, but from God's sovereign will.

While Moses's humility is evident in his self-assessment and willingness to serve, his authority is equally unmistakable throughout the narrative. This divine authority emerges from several sources. When God first speaks to Moses, He assigns him an authoritative role to confront a mighty Pharaoh and deliver an entire people from bondage (Exodus 3:10, NKJV). The authority given to Moses is not contingent upon human credentials but is a direct commission from the Almighty.

As Moses embarks on his mission, God equips him with signs, turning his staff into a serpent, inflicting plagues upon Egypt, and eventually parting the Red Sea (Exodus 7-14). These miracles serve to validate Moses's authority in the eyes of both his people and his adversaries. Perhaps the most compelling evidence of Moses's authority is his unique relationship with God. Numbers 12:6-8 (NKJV) emphasizes that Moses speaks with God "face to face," in contrast to the more mediated revelations granted to other prophets. This close communion underscores that Moses was not merely a man but a leader entrusted with the highest level of divine insight.

The interplay between humility and authority in Moses's character is thus a dynamic tension that defines his leadership. He constantly reminds the Israelites that his strength and, by extension, their deliverance, rest on God alone. His humility ensures that his authority is used to serve, not to lord over others, and his willingness to intercede on behalf of his people further establishes him as a compassionate leader.

To understand how Moses balanced humility with authority, it is helpful to examine pivotal moments recorded in the NKJV. The Burning Bush (Exodus 3:1-12): Moses encounters a bush that burns without being consumed. God commands him to remove his sandals because "the place where you stand is holy ground" (Exodus 3:5, NKJV). The holiness of the ground symbolizes the sacred nature of the task Moses is about to undertake. Yet, Moses's reaction is one of humility; he conceives that he is unworthy, remarking on his insignificance relative to the monumental task ahead. Here, God does not rebuke Moses for his humble attitude; rather, He uses it to reinforce His point: human frailty is the very context in which divine power operates.

In another key moment, Moses's hesitancy, his self-questioning, and his low self-perception contrast strikingly with the authority that God bestows upon him. Through this encounter, Moses learns that true power does not stem from self-reliance but from surrendering to God's will. The burning bush becomes a symbol not only of God's miraculous power but also of the sanctity that accompanies divine mission, a combination that enabled Moses to embody humility and authority simultaneously.

No episode better illustrates Moses's balancing act than his confrontations with Pharaoh. (Exodus 5-12). When Moses and his brother Aaron stand before Pharaoh demanding the release of the Israelites, Pharaoh's defiant questioning sets the stage for an extraordinary display of both humility and divine authority. In these interactions, Moses does not rely solely on his eloquence or personal strength; instead, he depends on God's power as evidenced by the plagues that follow. For example, in Exodus 7:1-2 (NKJV), God declares to Moses, "See, I have made you a god to Pharaoh, and Aaron your brother shall be your prophet." Here, the use of the word "god" reflects the extraordinary responsibility Moses carries. Yet, it is crucial to note that Moses's authority is not self-generated; it is merely a channel through which God's sovereign will is revealed. Even as Moses stands before the Egyptian king, his demeanor reflects his humble awareness that he acts only on God's behalf. His consistency in attributing all success to divine intervention bolsters the Israelites' faith and reinforces the idea that true authority is tempered by a servant's heart.

Furthermore, leading in the Wilderness (Exodus 16–17, Numbers 14, Deuteronomy 1-3) exemplifies Moses's ability to combine humility with authoritative action. Leading a people in transition, fraught with rebellion, discontent, and uncertainty, requires a leader who not only commands respect but also listens and intercedes. When the Israelites complain about the bitter water at Marah or grumble about the lack of food, Moses frequently turns to prayer and intercession. Even after the incident of the golden calf (Exodus 32), when the people's sin incites God's wrath, Moses boldly intercedes on their behalf (Exodus 32:11-14, NKJV). His intercession reveals a heart that bears the people's pain, yet does so with humility that never places him above them. It also underscores his role as a mediator, one who uses his divinely granted authority to secure mercy rather than to impose judgment. In Numbers 14, following the discouraging report by the spies, the people want to return to Egypt, yet Moses firmly stands by the faith of God's promise. In these moments, Moses demonstrates that his authority does not isolate him from the struggles of his people; instead, it compels him to support, educate, and guide them on the path set by God.

Perhaps one of the most profound lessons from Moses's life is the realization that divine power is perfected in human weakness. This idea is also echoed in the New Testament (2 Corinthians 12:9). Moses's humility, his willingness to admit, "I am not eloquent" (Exodus 4:10, NKJV), is not a sign of defeat but a revealing of his true strength. In that moment, the reader is reminded that when a leader encounters his own limitations, he can rely on God's limitless strength. This principle invites modern believers and leaders alike to refrain from an over-reliance on personal ability and instead to trust in a power far greater than themselves.

Moses's authoritative acts, from issuing direct commands to negotiating with powerful rulers, are consistently aligned with his commitment to serve the people rather than to dominate them. His leadership demonstrates that authority, when exercised with humility, becomes an instrument for building community and advocating for others. In today's environment, whether in business, government, or spiritual communities, there is often a tension between those who seek power for its own sake and those who use authority to foster uplifting transformations. Moses stands as a testimony that true authority derives its strength from a selfless trust in God and an ongoing commitment to the welfare of others. He shows leaders that power should be used to serve and care for those they lead. He mastered the duality well!

In today's world, where leadership challenges often border on the transactional rather than transformational, Moses's example is both a beacon and a challenge. It invites every leader or aspiring leader to measure success not solely by the accumulation of power or achievement of goals but by the degree to which they serve others with compassion, integrity, and humility. Ultimately, Moses's legacy teaches us that when authority is intertwined with humility, the impact of leadership becomes enduring and transformative.

May we, in our various spheres of influence, emulate this balance by remembering that true authority is born out of a humble heart, a heart that is open to learning, ready to serve, and devoted to a higher purpose. In doing so, we not only lead with effectiveness but also inspire those around us to live lives marked by the same blend of reverence and courage that defined Moses's extraordinary journey. Ultimately, Moses's life is a timeless testament to the power of balancing humility with authority. His story continues to offer guidance for anyone who aspires to lead with integrity, compassion, and unwavering conviction. As we reflect on his example, let us commit to cultivating both the humility that fosters deep connections and the authority that empowers change!

Chapter 5-The Maturity of the Man

One of the most dramatic episodes in the history of Israel is the parting of the Red Sea (Exodus 14). With the Egyptian army closing in, the Israelites found themselves trapped between certain death and the unknown wilderness on the other side of the sea. In this moment of extreme crisis, the maturity of Moses shone brightly.

You know the story, the Israelites cry out in fear as they realize the severity of their predicament. Pharaoh's relentless pursuit left them with little hope. Against this backdrop, God spoke to Moses, commanding him to "lift up your staff, and stretch out your hand over the sea, and divide it" (Exodus 14:16 NKJV). Moses's obedience transformed a hopeless situation into one of the most celebrated deliverances in Biblical history. A life matured by intimacy empowered him to do so! Let's explore.

Despite the urgency of the moment, Moses maintained a calm demeanor. His leadership demonstrated how tension can be defused through trust and decisive action. His ability to keep his own fears in check and focus on the task set by God was critical in instilling confidence among the people. A less mature man would have crumbled under this weight. By obeying God's command, Moses became an instrument through which the miraculous power of God was displayed. The parting of the Red Sea not only allowed the Israelites to escape but also served as an indelible sign of God's protection and intervention. This miracle was a potent reminder that, despite their dire circumstances, the God of Israel was actively fighting on their behalf.

Reflecting on the Red Sea episode, it becomes clear that leadership in crisis is not solely about overcoming immediate threats but also about manifesting trust and encouraging communal confidence, sure signs of maturity. Moses's example teaches us that during times of overwhelming adversity, leaders must remain anchored in their faith and act decisively even when the path forward is shrouded in uncertainty. His actions remind us that every crisis holds within it the seed of transformation, a call to trust in higher guidance, and to don the mantle of maturity for the benefit of the community.

Another significant moment that tested Moses's maturity was the commission to deal with the sin of idolatry after the incident of the Golden Calf (Exodus 32). This passage provides a vivid portrait of crisis within a community when fear and impatience lead to a wholesale rejection of the covenant. Recall, while Moses was on Mount Sinai receiving the Law from God, the Israelites, feeling abandoned and uncertain, persuaded Aaron to create a god from the people's gold (Exodus 32:1-4 NKJV). The resulting golden calf became the focal point of a collective rebellion, as the people celebrated with revelry, forsaking their covenant relationship with God. When Moses descended and witnessed the debauchery and idolatry, his response was one of righteous indignation. In Exodus 32:19 NKJV, it is recorded that Moses "heard the sound of the people... and he burned with anger, and he threw the tablets from his hands and broke them at the foot of the mountain." This reaction was not merely an emotional lapse; it represented a deep sorrow for the broken trust between God and His people, a reflection of Moses's personal anguish over their shared failure. Here is where maturity prevailed:

Moses did not shy away from confronting the sin head-on. His dramatic reaction demonstrated that betrayal of God's commandments was unacceptable, even in a crisis. This decisive confrontation was essential in re-orienting the community's focus back to God.

Perhaps one of the most striking features of Moses's mature leadership in this episode is found in his intercessory prayer. After witnessing the store of disobedience among the Israelites, Moses beseeched God to forgive them: "Yet now, if You will forgive their sin, but if not, please blot me, I pray, out of Your book which You have written" (Exodus 32:32 NKJV). This act of self-sacrifice and humility underscored his commitment to his people and his role as a mature mediator.

Maturity in Crisis Management Beyond Miracles

While the miraculous deliverances, such as the Red Sea parting and the intervention during the Golden Calf crisis, are the more dramatic manifestations of Moses's maturity, there is also a subtler but equally powerful side to his maturity — the management of day-to-day crises within the community.

Moses frequently encountered dissent and complaints among the Israelites. For example, during the long wilderness journey, the people expressed frustration over the lack of food and water (see Exodus 16 and 17). In these episodes, Moses often served as a mediator, addressing practical concerns while reinforcing the need for trust in God's provision.

How did this exemplify his maturity? Rather than responding with immediate anger, Moses consistently turned to God for guidance. When faced with complaints about manna (Exodus 16), his leadership was characterized by a calm assurance that God would sustain them. In Numbers 11, although Moses himself grew weary under the burden of managing numerous complaints, his appeals to God for assistance and his willingness to delegate responsibilities (as advised by his father-in-law Jethro in Exodus 18) highlight an evolution in his leadership style. Nothing exposes the lack of maturity more than the pressure of crises. How a leader manages a crisis is one of the most reliable metrics of maturity.

One of the most significant insights into crisis management is found in the delegation of responsibilities. Exhausted by trying to personally resolve all disputes among the people, Moses accepted Jethro's original advice to establish a system of judges over the people. This not only distributed the burden but also empowered others in the community to take on leadership roles, thereby encouraging a sense of shared responsibility and trust. Further, Moses's leadership was underpinned by his consistent and clear communication. In moments of crisis, his willingness to speak truth, both in challenging the stubbornness of the people and in standing before God, established his reputation as a leader who did not falter under pressure.

When dealing with transgressions, Moses displayed a balance between justice and mercy. His stern reaction to the Golden Calf incident shows a commitment to upholding the covenant, yet his intercession on behalf of his people demonstrates his profound compassion. This dual approach ensured that while disobedience was met with serious accountability, it was also met with the hope of forgiveness and restoration.

There is a timeless lesson in these narratives: effective crisis management requires both a strategic vision and the humility to involve others in the process. Effectively executing both requires a mature man. Moses's willingness to delegate and communicate clearly with his people is an enduring testament to the power of collaborative leadership. In today's organizational settings, leaders can learn from Moses's example by embracing transparency, admitting vulnerabilities, and empowering others to share the burden of crisis. In reflecting on Moses's journey to maturity, several revelatory insights emerge that are pertinent to both personal spiritual growth and contemporary leadership:

First, throughout his life, Moses exhibited an unwavering reliance on God. Whether standing before Pharaoh (Exodus 5-10) or interceding for a rebellious nation (Exodus 32), he modeled his understanding of this principle: divine wisdom surpasses human limitations.

Second is the power of resilience. The wilderness journey was not a period of ease for the Israelites; it was characterized by physical hardships and emotional turmoil. Moses's perseverance, even when weary and under immense pressure, teaches the importance of resilience. His narrative suggests that enduring trust in times of crisis is built through consistent, patient leadership that neither avoids difficult decisions nor shirks responsibility.

Next, one of Moses's most profound contributions as a leader was his role as an intercessor. His willingness to plead for his people even to the point of offering himself (Exodus 32:32) highlights a selfless aspect of leadership. This intercessory role emphasizes that leaders are often called to stand in the gap for others, offering hope and a path to reconciliation.

All in all, Moses's journey demonstrates that crises often serve as catalysts for transformation. The miracles associated with crisis moments, the parting of the Red Sea and the provision of manna, are not just historical events; they symbolize how divine intervention can turn desperate situations into opportunities for renewal. For modern readers, this is an invitation to see challenges as moments where faith is deepened and communities are re-forged in the fires of adversity. Moses may have started as a reluctant man, plagued by imposter syndrome, but his journey matured him into a transformed vessel, fit for the Master's use.

Part
TWO
The Messenger

Chapter 6- Moses: The Lawgiver

In evaluating Moses's role as Lawgiver, one must appreciate the dual nature of his ministry. On one hand, his authority was divinely conferred and reinforced through acts of supernatural intervention, while on the other, his personal humility and willingness to intercede on behalf of his people demonstrate a deep commitment to righteousness and grace. Moses's role as lawgiver is a balance between divine authority and personal humility. Journey with me up to Mount Sinai, where he mediates God's laws, including the Ten Commandments, establishing a framework for justice, mercy, and holiness. His intercessory prayers and leadership emphasize that the law is both a moral blueprint and a call to a transformative relationship with God. Let's see how Moses's humility and authority serve as a model for servant leadership grounded in righteousness and compassion.

The dramatic setting of Mount Sinai, described in Exodus 19, 20, and 24, is where Moses emerges not only as a leader but as a lawgiver, the mediator between God and humankind. The Israelites, having been recently delivered from Egyptian bondage, gather at the foot of the mountain. There, amidst awe-inspiring natural phenomena (thunder, lightning, and the sound of a trumpet as recorded in Exodus 19:16-19), the people witness firsthand the holiness of God.

In Exodus 20, God speaks to the people and delivers the Decalogue, commonly known as the Ten Commandments, which constitute the core moral instructions for Israel. The commandments were not a list of arbitrary rules; they were divine directives that provided a blueprint for living in a community defined by justice, mercy, and holiness. Moses's role in this context was pivotal. He stood as the interlocutor between God's transcendent holiness and the sinful, fragile nature of humanity. When Moses descended from the mountain bearing the tablets (Exodus 32:15-19), the shattered tablets symbolized not only the Israelites' disobedience but also the high cost of failing to honor the covenant. He became the Lawgiver.

Purpose of the Law

The laws given through Moses provided a comprehensive framework covering not only religious observance but also social justice, interpersonal relationships, and economic fairness. In Exodus 21-23, Moses outlines laws concerning slavery, restitution, and the treatment of strangers, regulations that were radical for their time. These laws were intended to establish a society based on the principles of fairness, compassion, and respect for life. By instituting such detailed precepts, God demonstrated concern for every facet of social order. For modern readers, these passages remind us that divine law is not merely about ritualistic observance; it is a profound blueprint for righteous living that touches every aspect of communal life.

A balance between strict justice and boundless mercy characterizes Moses's presentation of the law. In Exodus 34, when God renews the covenant after the incident with the Golden Calf, the renewed tablets reveal that while God's standards are unyielding, His willingness to forgive remains ever-present. Moses himself exemplifies this balance. When the people sin, Moses is quick to intercede. His famous plea in Exodus 32:32, "Please blot me out of Your book which You have written," illustrates a heart wholly poured out in intercession, reflecting his understanding that the law is as much about restoring as it is about punishing disobedience.

The covenant, codified by the law, was not an end but rather a means to cultivate a disciplined, orderly society, a people who would reflect God's holiness on earth. In Deuteronomy, Moses reiterates the necessity of obeying God's commandments in order to receive His blessings (Deuteronomy 28). This connection between obedience and divine favor is central to understanding the law's purpose. It was not simply a system of rules but a call to enter into a transformative relationship with God, one that would redefine every aspect of life. For Moses, imparting the law was an act of establishing divine order. It was a sacred duty to see that the people lived in a way that would mark them as God's treasured possession.

The Humble Lawgiver

His humility repeatedly characterizes Moses. Despite his position as the intermediary of God's law, he often laments his shortcomings. For instance, in Numbers 12, when his siblings challenged his authority, Moses humbly accepted God's affirmation of his unique role while also expressing personal sorrow. This humility is crucial because it models a form of leadership that is not autocratic but rather prioritizes service. Moses's humility invites others to approach God honestly and without pretension, a necessary quality in a community that is trying to rein in the sins of pride and self-righteousness.

At the same time, Moses was charged with enormous authority. He was expected to speak with God's voice, deliver judgments, and sometimes even discipline the people with an iron hand. For example, when the Israelites rebelled after the Golden Calf incident, Moses exercised his God-given authority to restore order. His actions in breaking the tablets symbolized a decisive break from sin and a call to renew the commitment to divine law. Moses was neither hesitant nor timid when it came to enforcing God's word. His authoritative acts were always tempered by the knowledge that he was acting under divine commission, a juxtaposition that grounds his authority in humility. In other words, his power was not self-generated but flowed from God, and he consistently made it known that he was merely God's representative.

The delicate balance Moses maintained between humility and authority offers crucial lessons for leaders today. His example teaches that true authority is not about dominating others but about serving them, about harnessing one's gifts to uplift a community. Leaders who acknowledge their own limitations, who continually seek God's guidance, and who willingly admit error when necessary can create environments of trust and accountability. Moses offers a model of servant leadership in which power is used responsibly and compassionately, ensuring that structures align with divine justice and mercy.

The NKJV renders the accounts with a formal respect toward the law that Moses delivered. Verses such as Exodus 20:1-17 (the Ten Commandments) are not just moral imperatives; they are divinely inspired decrees that carry the weight of God's own authority. Reading these passages, one is struck by the way the law was meant to function as a reflection of God's character: holy, just, merciful, and loving. The solemn tone of these declarations reminds us that the law is meant to be a mirror, showing us both our shortcomings and the ideal toward which we are called. For believers, internalizing these laws means internalizing God's heart and striving to reflect His righteousness in daily life.

Moses's life calls us to reflect personally on the cost of obedience. His willingness to stand against the rebellious tendencies of the Israelites, even when it meant personal sacrifice, challenges modern believers to evaluate how they live out their own faith. The NKJV's narrative style, with its rich detail and reverence for divine encounters, offers a model for personal accountability. Moses's intercessions and moments of deep vulnerability (as seen in his pleas during the Golden Calf incident) invite us to be honest about our own failures while trusting in God's unfailing grace. His life epitomizes that obedience is not blind submission but a dynamic, ongoing engagement with God's word. In this way, Scripture becomes a tool for molding character, fostering a spirit that is both humble before God and confident in His guidance.

An often-overlooked aspect of Moses's ministry is the quiet, sustaining presence of the Holy Spirit. In passages where Moses's strength seems to falter, we see hints of divine enablement that carried him through challenges. The Spirit not only emboldened him to confront Pharaoh and lead an entire nation but also gently reminded him of his dependence on God. This interplay between divine empowerment and personal humility teaches that true authority comes not from our own abilities but from our reliance on God. The NKJV accounts, by preserving the sanctity of these interactions, encourage believers to seek this same balance of empowerment and meekness in their own lives.

The example of Moses as Lawgiver directly informs modern conceptions of leadership, especially for those in faith-based contexts. Leaders today can learn from his example by:

- Acting decisively in the face of injustice or sin, knowing that authority without accountability can lead to abuse.
- Remaining accessible and humble, ensuring that power is never wielded to intimidate but rather to uplift and guide.
- Embodying the principles of divine law by ensuring that practices in organizations or communities reflect justice, mercy, and righteousness.

Beyond organizational leadership, Moses's model challenges believers to organize their personal lives in ways that honor divine order. This might include:

- Developing personal routines that incorporate Scripture reading, prayer, and self-examination, akin to Moses's regular encounters with God.
- Being intentional about cultivating character traits such as patience, integrity, and compassion, virtues that underpin the commandments and reflect the character of God.
- Engaging in community accountability, where peers or mentors help ensure that one's conduct aligns with the values taught in Scripture.

Moses's heartfelt intercessions for his people serve as a blueprint for the power of prayer. His willingness to put the welfare of his nation above his own needs and even risk personal damnation underscores the vital role of intercessory prayer in maintaining a bond between God and His people. In practical terms, believers are called to:

- Pray regularly for their communities and leaders.
- Embrace personal sacrifice in the service of others, reflecting the servant heart of Moses.
- Seek to mediate conflicts and encourage reconciliation, modeling the restorative work of the law.

Moses, as Lawgiver, stands as a monumental figure who exemplified both the weight of divine authority and the humility necessary to wield that authority rightly. The NKJV scriptures paint a picture of a man who, despite his own shortcomings, was bestowed with the responsibility to communicate God's perfect law, a law that not only governed the behavior of the Israelites but also set the standard for divine order on earth.

The balance Moses maintained between strictness and compassion, judgment and mercy, authority and humility serves as a timeless lesson for every believer called to leadership. His life reminds us that the mandate to lead according to God's standards is inseparable from the call to humble service. As we reflect on Moses's encounters at Sinai, his intercessory prayers, and even his moments of personal vulnerability, we are challenged to adopt a similar posture in our own lives.

In a world often marked by the abuse of power and the erosion of moral standards, Moses's legacy calls us back to the foundational principles of divine order. His example teaches that true leadership is not about self-aggrandizement but about faithfully transmitting God's word, building communities rooted in justice and mercy, and, above all, trusting in the sustaining power of God. As leaders, whether in our families, communities, or places of work, we are invited to balance our authority with humility, to speak as conduits of divine truth, and to consistently reflect the character of our Lord.

Thus, Moses remains not only a historical figure but also a profound model of faith-driven leadership, whose life continues to inspire and guide those who seek to administer God's law with integrity and compassion. In embracing his example, we learn that the call to serve is as much about personal transformation and self-examination as it is about showing and maintaining the divine order that binds us together as a community of believers.

In summary, Moses as Lawgiver offers a multifaceted portrait: a man empowered by God who bore the burden of divine commandments and, through both humility and authority, laid down principles that continue to influence ethical, social, and spiritual systems across generations. His life invites every believer to consider how divine law is not only to be heard and obeyed but also to be lived out with grace and compassion, a legacy that remains as relevant today as it was at the foot of Sinai.

Chapter 7- Moses: The Mediator

Being in covenant with the Creator of all, can be a big ask. For God's chosen people, Israel, navigating this new relationship required a bridge. But not just any mediator would do. This assignment required one anointed for the task – Moses. His encounter at the burning bush (Exodus 3) marks the beginning of a mission that would define Israelite's identity. Called by God to lead His people out of Egypt, Moses becomes a figure of trust for both God and the Israelites.

The covenant at Mount Sinai stands as a seminal moment in Israelite history. In Exodus 19 and 20, we read of God descending upon the mountain in fire and thunder, delivering the Ten Commandments, which form the bedrock of the Mosaic law. This event signifies that the relationship between God and Israel is not arbitrary; it is grounded in divine order and covenantal obligation.

The significance of this covenant lies in its comprehensive nature. It established a legal, priestly, and ethical framework that was designed to transform an ex-slave people into a nation devoted to living standards that reflected God's character. The laws given covered every aspect of life, from personal morality to communal justice, ensuring that community behavior was regulated by principles intended to mirror the holiness of God.

Moses's role extended beyond delivering the law. His personal experiences with God, such as his intimate dialogues in which God outlines the conditions for blessing and cursing (Deuteronomy 28), positioned him as the ultimate teacher and exemplar. The law was not given as a mere set of rules but as a covenant of relationship that required engagement, reverence, and heartfelt obedience.

Covenantal Relationships

A covenant, in its biblical sense, is a binding agreement that establishes rights and obligations. In Moses's narrative, God takes the initiative. By reaching out to His people, He transforms them from a scattered group of former slaves into a chosen nation. This covenant is not based solely on the actions of the people but is rooted in God's unchanging love and sovereign purpose.

The NKJV scriptures are replete with references to God's promises contingent on obedience. The covenant, as articulated in Exodus and Deuteronomy, outlines blessings for obedience and curses for disobedience. For instance, Deuteronomy 28 sets forth detailed promises of prosperity if the covenant is upheld and warns of severe consequences should the people deviate from the divine mandates. This covenantal arrangement is reminiscent of a formal contract, but it is one imbued with grace because it originates with a perfect God who always looks to restore rather than to simply punish.

Central to the covenant is the relational dynamic between God and His people. It is not a sterile legal document but a living relationship founded on mutual commitment. God's law calls for love both for God and for one's neighbor. When Jesus later summarizes the Law and the Prophets as loving God with all one's heart, soul, and mind (Matthew 22:37-40), it echoes Moses's teachings about loving and obeying God as the essence of a true covenant relationship.

The covenant solidified Israel's identity. The laws provided a counter-cultural stance against the prevalent customs of the ancient Near East, anchoring the community in practices that underscored purity, justice, and sanctification. From dietary prohibitions to rituals of sacrifice, every ceremonial and civil regulation was intended to distinguish God's people from the surrounding nations and to set them on a path toward communal holiness.

The Mosaic Law includes a wide array of commandments that govern ethical interactions among people. The Ten Commandments, for example, address the relationship between the individual and God as well as interpersonal relationships. Laws regarding honesty, respect for parents, prohibition of murder, and other moral imperatives lay the foundation for a safe and just society.

Beyond moral imperatives, the Mosaic laws were practical in their orientation. They covered various aspects of daily life, from property rights and marriage customs to the responsibilities of judges and the treatment of foreigners. For instance, Exodus 22 outlines instructions about restitution and compensation, reflecting a system of justice that emphasizes restoration over unmerited retribution. Such laws were instrumental in creating social order and resolving conflicts in the community.

The statutes regarding worship, sacrifices, festivals, and priesthood were key components of the covenant. The prescribed rituals were not only acts of worship but also continual reminders to the Israelites of their special relationship with God. The regular observances served as communal markers of identity and reinforced the covenant in the everyday lives of the people.

The laws given through Moses also foreshadow the coming of the prophets, who later called for a return to the true spirit behind the law, justice, mercy, and love (Micah 6:8). While the laws themselves provided structure, the heart of the covenant was always meant to be a transformation of character. The prophetic texts often highlight that legalistic observance without true justice and compassion is unacceptable to God. Thus, the legal system operated as a scaffold, guiding the community until individuals matured in spirit and righteousness.

The Mosaic Law was a temporary arrangement that would pave the way for the more universal covenant revealed in Christ. Nevertheless, the principles embedded within these laws, justice, accountability, and care for others, remain relevant today. The legal codes established a precedent for many modern systems of justice and ethics. Even though Christians now live under the New Covenant of grace through faith in Jesus Christ, the ancestral laws serve as a testament to God's enduring concern for holy living and just society.

Context of NKJV Passages

Understanding the context of these passages is crucial. The NKJV translation preserves the rich historical and cultural backdrop within which these laws were delivered. Israel, at the time of Moses, was emerging from the oppressive conditions of Egypt, a setting that necessitated a radical reorientation of life. The Israelites had to transition from a state of servitude to one of nationhood, with new legal systems that would define their identity.

The ancient Near East was characterized by diverse religions and customs. For Israel, the laws encapsulated a unique monotheistic belief system centered on a singular, omnipotent God. The NKJV passages underline that the laws were not arbitrary human inventions, but divinely instituted guidelines designed to lead the people on a path of holiness and distinctiveness.

When the laws were given at Sinai, it was not done secretly. Instead, they were shouted from the mountaintop, read aloud, and inscribed on stone tablets. Such a public declaration emphasized that the covenant was a communal commitment. Every member of the community, from the elders to the servants, was called to abide by these precepts. As recorded in Exodus 24 and Deuteronomy 5, this public aspect of the covenant signified that rules were binding on everyone, highlighting the communal nature of the relationship between God and Israel.

The rituals and symbols embedded in these passages were designed to be both instructive and formative. The use of water during the crossing of the Red Sea, the smoke and fire of Sinai, and the ritual feasts all pointed to deeper spiritual truths regarding purification, divine intervention, and the sustaining presence of God. Each symbol and each command about ritual practice was intended to remind the Israelites of their covenant obligations and reinforce the sacredness of their daily lives.

One of the most striking personal insights from these passages is the sense of awe and reverence that they evoke. The NKJV brings out vivid depictions of divine majesty - fire, thunder, and the very sound of God's voice.

These expressions remind believers that the laws are not mere regulations but encounters with the holiness of God. For many readers, this inspires a spiritual longing to live in a way that is pleasing to God, motivating them to adopt a lifestyle centered on worship and obedience.

Personal transformation is a recurrent theme in the covenant. The call to obey God's laws is not a call to legalism but an invitation to a transformed life. This perspective resonates deeply with the Christian understanding of sanctification, whereby believers are continuously shaped in the likeness of Christ. In the NKJV, Moses's repeated exhortations to adhere to the covenant "with all your heart" challenge every believer to examine their inner life and strive for integrity, sincerity, and complete devotion to God.

Another profound insight is the dynamic interplay between justice and mercy found within the laws. While the Mosaic laws prescribe penalties for transgressions reflecting the serious nature of sin, they also make provisions for mercy and forgiveness. This balance foreshadows the redemptive work of Christ, who embodies both justice in His righteousness and mercy in His sacrificial love. Personal reflection on these passages often leads believers to appreciate that God's laws are not punitive but intended for the holistic restoration of the individual and, by extension, the community.

For contemporary readers, the laws of Moses, though ancient, offer timeless truths applicable to modern life. The call to social justice, the importance of community accountability, and the emphasis on ethical behavior are as relevant today as they were in ancient Israel. Scriptures such as Leviticus 19 ("You shall love your neighbor as yourself") continue to resonate, serving as a moral compass in an increasingly complex world. This motivational aspect of the covenant encourages believers to pursue lives marked by compassion, fairness, and a deep respect for all human dignity.

Many find comfort in the covenantal framework because it accounts for the human condition, flawed, prone to sin, yet capable of redemption. The NKJV recounts multiple instances in which the Israelites' failure to live up to the law is met with God's enduring faithfulness and an opportunity for repentance. This cyclical pattern of falling away and returning to God provides a powerful message of hope. Personal insights often include reflections on one's own failures and the transformative grace available through genuine repentance and commitment to God's ways.

A recurring revelation from these passages is that divine law is intrinsically connected to God's love. Far from being a set of arbitrary rules, the law is an expression of God's care for His creation. By delineating ethical boundaries and communal responsibilities, God manifests His concern for justice, peace, and mutual respect among His people. This perspective not only elevates the law from a set of prohibitions to one of divine love but also serves as an ongoing reminder that every human interaction should reflect God's character. Reading these passages, many believers are inspired to view the law as a guide to nurturing relationships that honor both God and one another.

The Legacy of the Covenant in Community Life

The establishment of the Mosaic covenant radically redefined what it meant to be part of a community. The laws served as a social contract that bound the people together, fostering an intense sense of identity rooted in shared beliefs and practices. This unity was crucial for survival, especially considering the challenges faced by a nation in a hostile environment. The legacy of this covenant is evident in the enduring cultural and religious identity of the Jewish people, a legacy that has influenced not only Judaism but also Christianity and Islam.

Many legal and ethical principles that originated with the Mosaic laws continue to influence modern legal systems. Concepts such as the sanctity of life, the right to a fair trial, and the importance of community support can be traced back to these ancient statutes. For modern communities, these principles offer a practical blueprint for addressing social issues, establishing equitable societies, and fostering environments where justice prevails.

A significant aspect of the covenant was its capacity to balance individual liberties with the welfare of the community. While the laws require personal responsibility, they also lay the groundwork for a collaborative effort to sustain social order. This balance is essential in today's world, where individualism often clashes with communal needs. The Mosaic covenant, as revealed in the NKJV, provides a framework that emphasizes generosity, accountability, and the importance of working together for the common good.

The covenant was designed never to be static. Throughout Israel's history, there were seasons of renewal when the community was called to recommit to its covenant with God. Modern believers can draw inspiration from these moments of recommitment and transformation, understanding that the journey of faith is a continuous process of moral and spiritual growth. Renewing one's commitment to God's law continues to be an important practice for ensuring that communities flourish in unity and purpose.

Moses's role as the mediator of God's covenant and law is a profound chapter in the biblical narrative, rich with theological and practical lessons for both individual believers and entire communities. The scriptures offer a tapestry of divine actions, relational commitments, and ethical guidance that have shaped not only ancient Israelite society but also today's moral landscape.

The covenant shown at Sinai is more than an ancient contract; it is a living reminder of the deep relationship between God and His people, characterized by both justice and mercy. The laws passed down through Moses continue to serve as a model for righteous community living, balancing individual rights and responsibilities with the needs of the collective.

The revelatory insights gleaned from these passages underscore the transformative power of God's law. They encourage us to pursue a life marked by reverence, ethical conduct, and a commitment to the principles of justice and love. In our modern world, where the issues of community and morality are still very present, returning to the core truths of the Mosaic covenant can motivate us to build societies that respect our common humanity and the divine calling to live together peacefully.

Ultimately, Moses's legacy invites us to view the law not as an outdated set of rules, but as a divine expression of God's love, a love that demands our highest devotion, transforms our communities, and redeems our lives. Whether one approaches these texts with historical curiosity, theological inquiry, or personal devotion, the covenant and its laws remain a timeless guide that directs us towards a life of true righteousness and unity under God.

In reflecting on these passages, one is reminded that every law given was an opportunity for the people to draw closer to God and one another. This timeless principle is as applicable today as it was during the wilderness journey of ancient Israel: a call to build relationships, seek justice, and live in a way that reflects the sacred covenant established by a loving and just Creator.

The study of Moses, covenantal relationships, and the role of laws in community behavior ultimately challenges us to ask: How can we, in our daily lives, manifest a commitment to the ethical standards and communal responsibilities that continue to define what it means to be God's people? This reflection not only honors the ancient tradition but also paves the way for personal and communal transformation in today's world.

By embracing these divine commands and the underlying spirit of the covenant, communities can experience the fullness of life that God intended, a life marked by justice, mercy, and unwavering love. The legacy of the Mosaic covenant then becomes not just a historical memory, but a living testament to the power of obedience and faithfulness to change lives and societies.

Through the detailed exploration above, we see that Moses is not only a historical figure but also a perennial symbol of hope, a mediator who brought God's will into the everyday lives of His people. The covenant and the laws given through him continue to inform and shape contemporary views on morality, leadership, and community behavior. Whether studied for their doctrinal insights or their practical applications in modern society, the Mosaic statutes invite us all to strive for a higher standard of living grounded in the divine love and justice that remains as relevant today as ever.

Chapter 8- Moses: The Governor

The Book of Exodus presents us with a profound narrative: the liberation of the Israelites from the harsh grip of Egyptian oppression, which sets the stage for Moses's leadership. The dramatic events surrounding the Ten Plagues, the parting of the Red Sea, and the ensuing wilderness journey are not only historical markers for the nation of Israel but also underline the principle of divine intervention in human affairs. In the NKJV, these narratives come alive through powerful imagery of God's voice, the thunder and lightning on Mount Sinai, and the burning bush, which all contribute to establishing Moses as a divinely appointed leader – Governor of God's chosen people. Moses's governance integrates divine law with practical leadership, establishing justice, protecting the vulnerable, and managing crises during the wilderness journey. His leadership demonstrates accountability, resilience, and compassionate governance, balancing discipline with mercy.

Moses's call to lead was marked by personal humility and extraordinary responsibility. In Exodus 3, we read of the burning bush where God calls Moses to act, saying, "Come now, and I will send you to Pharaoh, that you may bring My people out of Egypt." This pivotal moment marks the beginning of a covenantal relationship based on obedience, trust, and the promise of a new identity rooted in holiness and divine law.

The covenant at Mount Sinai is perhaps one of the most significant moments in the Bible. Here, God outlines a series of laws intended to guide every facet of Israelite life from personal moral behavior to community, economic, and religious practices. The NKJV describes this event with grandeur: God descending upon the mountain with a thunderous voice, smoke, and fire (Exodus 19-20). The Ten Commandments are given as a concise codex of ethical imperatives that lay the foundation for justice and righteousness.

This covenant was meant to create a society distinct from surrounding cultures, one in which justice, mercy, and reverence for God governed not just the private domain but also public life. The laws were intended to elevate communal behavior, ensuring that personal virtue was closely tied to societal well-being. The covenant, therefore, was not merely a series of religious rituals; it was a comprehensive governance framework that continues to speak to modern discussions on law, ethics, and the role of government.

Moses's leadership is encapsulated in his role as lawgiver. He not only delivered God's commandments but also translated these divine instructions into a societal blueprint. In a modern context, Moses's example as an intermediary converting divine will into practical legislation mirrors the relationship between moral philosophy and secular law. The NKJV's portrayal of his struggle, humility, and occasional self-doubt (e.g., Exodus 4:10, when Moses questioned his capability) resonates with modern leaders who must navigate complex social, economic, and ethical challenges.

Moses's ability to communicate authority while remaining accessible to his people mirrors the foundation of modern democratic leadership, responsible public servants who interpret higher ideals and aspirations into actionable public policies. For instance, just as Moses convened assemblies and engaged in mediation during disputes (as seen in Numbers 11 and 16), contemporary leaders and legislatures work to reconcile conflicting interests within a pluralistic society.

At the heart of Moses's legislation lies a commitment to justice and equity. The legal codes found in Exodus, Leviticus, and Deuteronomy emphasize fairness. Laws concerning restitution, such as those in Exodus 22, required that those who wronged another make reparations to restore balance. This emphasis on restorative justice offers a rich parallel to modern legal systems that increasingly focus on rehabilitation over retribution.

Moses also set forth principles about protecting the vulnerable: widows, orphans, and foreigners were endangered groups afforded special consideration. In modern governance, these directives translate into welfare policies, human rights protections, and inclusive governance that ensures the integrity of all citizens. Modern policymakers often grapple with similar challenges: balancing the rule of law with social programs that support disadvantaged groups. Moses's statutes thus continue as a model for compassionate governance.

The wilderness journey was replete with challenges: scarcity of resources, rebellions, and internal dissent. Moses's leadership during these crises teaches modern leaders the importance of accountability and resilience. In instances such as the golden calf episode (Exodus 32), Moses demonstrated both firm discipline and the need for mercy. The prophetic rebuke that followed his intercession (Exodus 32:11-14) underscores that adherence to moral absolutes is essential even during times of social upheaval.

Modern governance frequently finds itself amid crises, whether economic downturns or social unrest, when decisive action, coupled with empathy, is needed. Moses's intercession on behalf of a rebellious nation invites modern leaders to consider the balance between legislative rigidity and the flexibility of mercy. His example underscores that true governance requires the courage to hold individuals accountable while also providing opportunities for redemption and transformation.

Biblical Insights & Modern Governance

One key insight from the Mosaic covenant is that governance is inherently relational. Unlike modern systems, which sometimes emphasize the separation of state and religion, the biblical model of governance ties the legitimacy of laws to a divine covenant. This means that the law is seen not merely as a set of prescriptions but as an expression of God's care for His people.

In modern societies, respecting human rights, establishing social safety nets, and promoting ethical leadership can be viewed as secular extensions of this covenantal principle. Although secular democracies may not invoke Moses directly, the underlying concept that legitimate authority is anchored in a commitment to the welfare of the people remains pertinent. Today's constitutions and legal frameworks, even in pluralistic societies, echo the idea that laws are a social contract born of a mutual commitment to justice, liberty, and equality.

The laws given to Moses encapsulate a comprehensive ethical framework that addresses the individual and the community. The NKJV passages emphasize that ethical behavior involves caring for our neighbors, an idea encapsulated in the commandment to "love your neighbor as yourself" (Leviticus 19:18). In modern ethical debates, especially those concerning social justice and public policy, this principle provides a robust foundation for advocating for equitable resource distribution, comprehensive healthcare, and environmental stewardship.

Modern governance can benefit from these biblical insights by emphasizing policies that nurture both individual responsibilities and the common good. The yearning for a society where law and morality are intertwined is reflected in movements that demand transparency, accountability, and fairness in public offices. Moses's example reminds us that effective governance requires policies that are diligent in upholding personal integrity and societal well-being alike.

The influence of Mosaic law extends beyond religious boundaries; it has helped shape the conceptual underpinnings of many modern legal systems. The Ten Commandments, for example, continue to represent a moral summa that has influenced Western legal and ethical thought. Principles such as the sanctity of life, property rights, and the necessity of truth and justice resonate in today's courtrooms and legislatures.

Modern constitutions, though secular, share similarities with the covenant at Sinai in that they are founded on principles believed to be intrinsic to human dignity and societal order. The idea that laws should promote not only individual freedom but also communal responsibility stands as a bridge between ancient and modern governance. It is within this continuum, a historical conversation between divine law and civil jurisprudence, that Moses's legacy finds new relevance.

The vivid depictions of divine majesty in the NKJV, whether it is God's powerful arrival at Sinai or Moses's experiences in the wilderness, serve as potent reminders of the accountability that leaders bear. For many modern believers, these passages evoke a sense of awe and a realization that leadership, in any form, should be exercised with the utmost respect for the responsibilities it entails. When leaders today draw from this tradition, they are reminded that authority comes not from power alone but from a commitment to serve a higher moral and ethical standard.

For example, many who study Moses's encounters at Sinai appreciate the symbolic transition from a disorganized, enslaved existence to one governed by divine order. This metaphor extends well to modern political systems, where the transition from chaos to order is seen as a fundamental goal of governance. In this light, Moses's legal and ethical codes serve as a reminder that laws should be tools for creating order, protecting rights, and ultimately fostering societal transformation.

As shared, Moses's narrative is one of personal transformation, of a hesitant man who grows into the mantle of leadership. Reflecting on these passages in the NKJV, many readers are inspired to examine their own paths toward personal and communal justice. Moses's initial reluctance and subsequent boldness exemplify that leadership is not inherent; it must be developed through experience, divine guidance, and a deep commitment to improvement.

This idea resonates strongly in contemporary society as well. Modern governance is increasingly recognizing that personal transformation for both leaders and citizens is vital for systemic change. Whether it is through educational reform, community outreach programs, or policy shifts aimed at reducing inequality, the journey toward justice remains a personal and collective one.

Moses's life teaches that transforming oneself is an essential step toward transforming society.

Another revelatory insight from the biblical narrative of Moses is the balance between maintaining tradition and adapting to modern realities. The Mosaic laws were revolutionary when given, yet adaptable enough to address the issues of their time. Today's legal and political frameworks face a similar challenge: respecting traditions that carry moral authority while adapting to society's evolving needs.

The NKJV passages invite personal reflection on the importance of cultural continuity alongside progressive governance. For instance, many communities today debate how to incorporate ancient ethical mandates, such as honesty, community service, and respect for life, into modern policies that address emerging challenges like digital privacy, climate change, and global migration. Moses's example shows that a foundational commitment to justice and compassion can serve as both an anchor and a guide, ensuring that, even in times of rapid change, society's core values remain protected.

Modern Governance in a Mosaic Framework

In Moses's legal system, justice was not an abstract ideal but a practical necessity. Laws were designed to mediate disputes, prevent exploitation, and ensure that every member of society, regardless of status, received fair treatment. Modern governance, too, demands systems that are not only efficient but also ethically grounded. From courts to legislative bodies, the principle that all citizens deserve impartial justice remains a cornerstone of democratic societies.

Policies informed by Mosaic principles can be found in modern legal ethics, including transparency in government institutions, equal protection under the law, and a commitment to remedying injustices. By looking at Moses's example, modern leaders are reminded that justice must always serve to uplift the collective, ensuring that all individuals can thrive in a supportive and equitable environment.

Moses's covenant was not a static set of rules but a living document meant to foster community and connection. It set forth responsibilities that, when honored, allowed society to flourish. In modern terms, a community can be seen as a living covenant where laws and policies are continually renewed through democratic participation. When citizens engage in the political process, they reaffirm their shared values much as the Israelites repeatedly renewed their covenant with God through rituals and public declarations.

This model has applications in modern governance. Practices such as public consultations, civic education programs, and community-based decision-making address the need for a participatory approach. They mirror the ancient practice where the community, united by a common vision and bound by divine law, navigated the complexities of social life. The scriptures remind us that community is built on a foundation of shared truths, mutual accountability, and ongoing dialogue.

The influence of Mosaic law is not confined to any single culture or nation; it has become a global touchstone for ethics, law, and governance. Many modern legal systems have drawn on these biblical principles, whether directly or indirectly, to establish norms in human rights, property law, and the separation of powers. The emphasis on accountability, communal responsibility, and the protection of the vulnerable resonates across diverse governance systems.

In our globalized world, the need for policies that bridge differences and promote inclusivity is paramount. Moses's legacy, as portrayed in the NKJV, reminds modern-day lawyers, judges, and policymakers that a commitment to justice must be universal. By advocating for policies that protect human dignity and uphold ethical standards, contemporary leaders echo the enduring wisdom of Moses's legal code.

Engaging with Moses's story in the NKJV can serve as a personal call to public service. The transitions Moses experienced, from being hesitant to stepping boldly into his role as leader, are emblematic of the personal growth required in any act of public engagement. Modern citizens are encouraged to see public service not as a burden, but as an honorable calling that mirrors the higher purpose of serving the community and advancing the common good. This reflection is as relevant today as it was in ancient times, urging each of us to contribute toward a just and equitable society.

On a personal level, the covenant Moses established with God transcends mere legalism; it is an invitation to a new way of life. For many believers, the NKJV's portrayal of this sacred relationship is a reminder that personal commitment to righteousness shapes not only individual lives but also entire communities. The covenant offers a model for interpersonal relationships built on trust, accountability, and unconditional love, qualities that are essential for effective governance and communal life. Personal insights drawn from this narrative propel an ongoing journey toward self-improvement and a more responsible, compassionate societal framework.

Finally, Moses's story encourages a meaningful integration of faith and civic duty. This integration challenges modern readers to consider the possibilities of inspired governance. In a world often divided by political ideologies and competing interests, Moses's legacy stands as a testament to the possibility of leadership that is both morally coherent and practically effective.

Moses's life and legacy, as depicted in the NKJV Scriptures, continue to influence discussions on governance, law, and societal transformation. From the historical exodus and the covenant at Sinai to modern debates on justice, equity, and community, Moses serves as an enduring model of leadership, responsibility, and faith. His role as a mediator between perfect divine law and the reality of human imperfection bridges the ancient and modern worlds.

Today, as policymakers grapple with complex issues such as inequality, human rights, and sustainable development, Moses's model resonates with renewed relevance. His journey underscores that authentic governance is not merely about wielding power but about stewarding resources, nurturing hope, and fostering an environment where justice prevails. It calls for a leadership style that is transparent, empathetic, and anchored in principles that transcend time.

By drawing on Moses's example, we are encouraged to envision modern governance as a living covenant, one that embraces the responsibilities of leadership, the dignity of every individual, and the pursuit of a society grounded in divine compassion and human accountability. As we integrate these ancient truths with contemporary challenges, Moses's timeless leadership continues to illuminate the path toward a more just, compassionate, and flourishing society.

Chapter 9- Moses: The Sent One

I n Exodus 3, Moses encounters God in the form of a burning bush, a moment that would forever mark the beginning of his journey as a leader. "Come now, and I will send you to Pharaoh, that you may bring My people, the children of Israel, out of Egypt" (Exodus 3:10 NKJV). Here, we witness the divine call that sets Moses apart not only as a liberator but as a person entrusted with a holy mission. This incident signals the importance of transparency in revelation: God does not hide His purpose but communicates it clearly. In an era where many "just went, instead of being sent," this facet of Moses's life is worth highlighting. Let's dive.

Moses's initial reluctance, citing his own inadequacies in Exodus 4:10, demonstrates a deep sense of accountability. Instead of taking the call lightly, Moses wrestles with his limitations, showing that ethical leadership begins with self-awareness and an honest appraisal of one's capabilities. This early interaction emphasizes that any leadership role requires both a personal and spiritual acknowledgment of responsibility.

Following the deliverance from Egypt, Moses ascended Mount Sinai, where God established His covenant with Israel. The dramatic events recorded in Exodus 19-20 reveal a scene charged with divine authority. Moses is entrusted with conveying the Ten Commandments, a set of ethical guidelines designed to promote justice, fairness, and communal accountability. The clear formulation of these laws underscores transparency: God's standards are made known to all, and there is no ambiguity regarding what is expected of the people.

Moses's role in receiving and reiterating these commandments not only highlights the importance of accountability in leadership but also serves as an example of how adherence to ethical conduct can transform an entire community. The Ten Commandments themselves stand as a testament to the idea that ethical behavior in both private and public life is non-negotiable for a well-ordered society.

Throughout the wilderness journey, Moses encounters numerous instances where his leadership is tested. One prominent example is the golden calf incident in Exodus 32. When the Israelites, in Moses's prolonged absence on Mount Sinai, fashioned and worshiped a golden calf, it was a direct violation of the covenant made with God. When Moses returned and saw the transgression, he did not shy away from accountability. Instead, he interceded passionately on behalf of his people, admitting their sin and pleading with God not to destroy them (Exodus 32:11-14 NKJV).

This episode highlights two crucial aspects of accountability. First is Moses's willingness to accept responsibility for the state of his people, even though he had been entrusted with their care. His intercession exemplifies a leader who does not hide behind bureaucratic detachment but stands in solidarity with his community, urging repentance and renewal. Second, Moses demonstrates moral courage by confronting the reality of sin and the ensuing consequences, thereby laying a foundation for a community committed to ethical reform.

Moses's humility is a recurring theme in the narrative of his leadership. In Numbers 12, when Miriam and Aaron challenge his authority, Moses responds not with anger, but with measured restraint and an openness to correction. The incident that led to Miriam's temporary removal illustrates that accountability in leadership means being open to scrutiny, even from one's closest associates. Moses's reaction to criticism reflects a transparent approach: he allows his leadership to be questioned and underscores that ethical leaders welcome accountability rather than fear it.

Furthermore, his consistent efforts to seek God's guidance in every decision-making process provide a blueprint for modern leaders. In moments of crisis, whether addressing rebellious factions or managing internal disputes, Moses is seen as a mediator who values open communication and responsible governance. His example shows that genuine humility and the willingness to admit one's shortcomings are essential qualities for maintaining trust, both within a community and in one's relationship with a higher authority.

One of the most striking examples of transparency in Moses's leadership is his public reading of the covenant. As recorded in Deuteronomy, Moses makes a point of reminding the Israelites of the covenant's terms and the reasons behind each law and command. This public declaration was not only an administrative act but a profound exercise in transparency, ensuring that every individual in the community was aware of their responsibilities and the divine rationale behind them.

In Deuteronomy 31, Moses instructs Joshua and the elders of Israel to be witnesses to the covenant, thereby institutionalizing a system of accountability for future generations. This act of documenting and sharing the covenant openly reinforces the ethical principle that leadership is not shrouded in secrecy but must be conducted with full disclosure. In doing so, Moses establishes that transparency is key to establishing lasting trust and fostering a sense of collective responsibility.

Moses is remembered not only for his administrative and judicial functions but also for leading by example. His personal lifestyle and choices, such as his moments of prayer, intercession, and adherence to God's commandments, demonstrate what it means to live an ethical life. When faced with the challenges of leadership, Moses does not impose laws from a distance; he lives them out, thereby inspiring his people to follow suit.

For example, despite the personal risks involved, Moses continuously advocates for the welfare of his people. His insistence on observing the Sabbath, maintaining communal rituals, and upholding fairness in all dealings communicates a personal commitment to the ethical standards he sets for the nation. Through his actions, Moses effectively communicates that ethical conduct is not optional but central to the identity of God's people. He was committed to doing what he was SENT to do, without compromise.

Moses's approach to justice is further illustrated in his balanced handling of transgressions. In instances of sin, his initial response is not solely punitive. Instead, Moses demonstrates an understanding of the complexities of human behavior by interceding for mercy while still upholding the seriousness of the transgression. This balance between justice and mercy is crucial for ethical leadership, as it ensures that discipline does not become oppressive while also maintaining accountability.

The narrative of the golden calf serves as a stark illustration. Although the people had sinned grievously, Moses's plea for forgiveness and his willingness to stand in the gap allowed for a tempered application of divine justice. This episode shows that ethical leadership requires the judgment to enforce strict standards while still leaving room for redemption. Leaders who demonstrate this balance are better able to create environments that encourage personal growth instead of despair.

Moses's life embodies the concept of servant leadership, a foundational idea in both biblical and modern leadership theories. Servant leadership emphasizes that a true leader's role is to serve others rather than to be served. As Moses consistently puts the needs of his people above his own, modern readers are reminded that responsibility and ethical conduct come from a heart of service. Make no mistake, a servant leader must be SENT.

Integrity is a thread that runs throughout Moses's story. From the moment he receives God's command at the burning bush to the establishment of laws at Sinai, Moses's actions consistently reflect adherence to a higher standard of conduct. This consistency is crucial in building trust among the people. Scripture shows that leaders who maintain integrity even when facing doubts or opposition can instill confidence and foster a culture of ethical behavior within their community. Those who are not sent will buckle eventually.

Applications of Moses's Leadership Principles

Today, the concept of accountability in leadership is highly valued in public office, corporate governance, and community organizations. Just as Moses held himself accountable for the actions of the Israelites, modern leaders must establish systems of checks and balances to ensure that policies are administered fairly. Whether it is through independent oversight committees, public audits, or transparent reporting systems, the principle is the same: leaders must answer to those they serve.

Moses's interactions, in which he frequently admitted his own limitations and sought counsel from God, serve as a powerful reminder that no one is infallible. Modern leaders can learn from this by fostering a culture where feedback is welcomed, mistakes are acknowledged, and corrections are made openly. The NKJV narrative supports this by showing how openness to accountability leads to collective healing and progress after communal failures.

Transparency in governance, much like the public declarations and written laws in Moses's time, is an essential pillar of trust. In today's digital age, the demand for transparency is more pronounced than ever. From government data to financial disclosures in the corporate world, stakeholders seek clear, unambiguous communication. Moses's practice of publicizing the covenant and ensuring that every law was available for scrutiny sets an early example of how leadership should operate in an open and accessible manner.

Modern applications of this principle include open government initiatives, publicly accessible records, and active engagement with community feedback. Leaders who emulate Moses's approach ensure that decisions made behind closed doors are scrutinized and validated by the broader community, thereby reinforcing ethical conduct and accountability.

The ethical conduct demonstrated by Moses offers a compelling model for leaders of any era. Whether navigating complex political landscapes or managing organizational dynamics, the lessons from Moses's life remind us that ethical leadership is not optional; it is a moral imperative. The Scriptures' vivid portrayal of divine justice and human frailty calls leaders to be transparent in their actions, accountable for their decisions, and unwavering in their commitment to truth and fairness.

For modern leaders, this means creating environments where integrity is rewarded, ethical dilemmas are addressed openly, and the welfare of the community is prioritized above personal gain. The enduring lessons of Moses guide us to pursue policies and practices that not only comply with legal standards but also reflect a higher calling toward righteousness and justice.

In our modern context, leaders across various sectors can draw inspiration from Moses's humble yet resolute character. Whether by instituting robust systems of accountability, practicing open communication, or leading by personal example, modern leadership continues to be shaped by the principles Moses championed. His balanced approach to justice, merging disciplinary integrity with compassionate intercession, provides a timeless framework that informs contemporary debates on ethical governance and responsible leadership. To pull off this combination effectively, being SENT is a must.

As we continue to navigate the challenges of modern leadership, the enduring lessons from Moses remind us that true power lies not in authority alone, but in the courage to be transparent, the resolve to be accountable, and the commitment to uphold ethical conduct in all aspects of life. His story is a living testament, inviting each of us to embrace a legacy of leadership that mirrors divine perfection, a legacy grounded in truth, justice, and love for humanity. It's not a call to be taken lightly.

Part
Three

The Mentor

Chapter 10- Lessons from the Man

I t has been said that a mentor gives you the gift of speed (Dr. Dharius Daniels). The life of a great mentor, such as Moses, offers numerous lessons that we can apply to accelerate our progress. Moses's transformation from reluctance to resolve, from shepherd to visionary, is not just a historical story; it offers timeless keys for leadership and ministry today. Let's lean into this great mentor and glean lessons from Moses, the Man.

To begin, Moses stands as an enduring example of how God can refine a man's imperfections into powerful testimonies of divine grace. His life illuminates the path from self-doubt to confident obedience, urging each of us to trust in the One who calls us beyond our limitations and into a future filled with purpose and promise.

Moses's initial hesitation underscores an important truth: God often chooses those who feel least capable. It is in our admission of weakness that God works to perfect our strengths. Don't overlook these mentor's nuggets:

- *Obedience is a Process:* The gradual progression from doubt to decisive action reminds us that growth in faith is an ongoing journey. Each step of obedience adds to our capacity to serve.
- *Divine Assurance Empowers Action*: The promise of God's presence is transformative. Knowing that we do not stand alone enables us to face even the gravest challenges.
- *Transformation Requires Trust*: Moses's story is a testimony to the fact that true transformation occurs when we trust God's plan, even when it seems overwhelming. The willingness to trust in divine strength can change not only our lives but also the lives of those we lead.

As a follower of Jesus, these lessons resonate deeply with me. Jesus Himself often called out the weaknesses of His disciples, choosing them not because they were the strongest but because He intended to demonstrate His power through their human frailties. Just as the encounter with the burning bush transformed Moses, we are invited to undergo a similar transformation through our relationship with Christ.

Reflecting on Moses's transformation, I see a mirror of the ongoing journey that every believer experiences. There have been moments when my own reluctance to step into God's plan threatened to keep me in the confines of self-doubt. However, the constant, reassuring presence of Jesus has served as a catalyst, turning hesitation into action and fear into faith.

Drawing from Moses's example, I am reminded to continually seek divine encounters that challenge and renew my understanding of purpose. His life reassures me that, regardless of how inadequate I may feel, God's strength is enough. The journey of faith is not about reaching perfection on our own, but about allowing God to shape us, step by step, into instruments of His will.

Moses's story is a clarion call for every believer: to listen for the voice of God in the quiet moments, to trust His promises fervently, and to rise above our insecurities with the confidence of divine backing. Each encounter with God, whether through Scripture, prayer, or the witnessing of miracles, serves as an opportunity to surrender our doubts and embrace the transformative love that calls us into action.

For me, and for all followers of Jesus, Moses serves as a profound reminder that divine transformation begins with a single, often unexpected encounter, a moment when God's voice pierces through a man's doubts and whispers, "I will certainly be with you." Embracing this truth transforms our reluctance into resilience, allowing us to step boldly into the destinies that God has prepared for us, as mighty men of valor.

Chapter 11- Lessons from the Wilderness Wanderer

The "wilderness" can be a scary place. These seasons in our lives are often marked by lack, loneliness, and languishing. Moses's journey through the wilderness provides timeless lessons for anyone struggling with adversity. The following insights, drawn from NKJV Scriptures, are as relevant today as they were for the Israelites centuries ago. In Exodus 13:21–22, we read about the pillar of cloud by day and the pillar of fire by night, which guided the Israelites through the uncharted wilderness. These manifestations of God's presence served many purposes:

- They assured the people that God was with them during every step of the journey.
- They provided divine direction in a land that was harsh and unfamiliar.
- They symbolized the active presence of God, making clear that even in the midst of uncertainty, His guidance is steadfast.

Today, when uncertainty and adversity cloud our vision, we can draw encouragement from Moses, the Mentor. Just as Moses responded to God's guidance - following the pillar of cloud by day and the pillar of fire by night - we too can choose to follow his example. Though we may not encounter visible signs as Moses did, we can discern God's leading through His Word, in prayer, and by seeking the wisdom of trusted mentors. When we encounter our own wilderness moments - whether through personal loss, professional challenges, or times of spiritual dryness - Moses's response calls us to trust in the promise of God's continual presence and to keep moving forward in faith.

Lesson: God's Provision Surpasses Our Limitations

Throughout the wilderness journey, Moses faced the people's constant complaints about a lack of food and water. Despite their grumbling, God responded with miraculous provision, manna from heaven (Exodus 16) and water from a rock (Exodus 17). Moses's leadership reveals that, while human resources are limited, God's power and generosity are boundless. We learn to trust that true life and sustenance come only from God.

Lesson: Dependence on God Is Wisdom, Not Weakness

By turning to God in times of need, Moses demonstrated that reliance on divine strength is not a sign of weakness, but an act of wisdom. He acknowledged that God's power exceeds our own, modeling a faith that rests not in self-sufficiency but in God's faithful provision.

Lesson: Gratitude Shifts Our Perspective

Moses taught the Israelites, and us, that in moments of struggle, it is essential to look beyond what we lack and focus on God's continual blessings. By cultivating daily gratitude and reliance on God, we experience His abundant grace. As Philippians 4:19 (NKJV) assures us, "All things are working together for good to those who love God," reminding us to trust in His ongoing provision.

More Insights from the Wilderness Wanderer

Transformation Through Trials

The wilderness served as a crucible for change, transforming the untamed nation of Israel into a people ready for the Promised Land. Moses himself grew from a hesitant shepherd into a powerful leader. The discipline required to endure hardships was essential to this process, as expressed in James 1:2–4 (NKJV): "Consider it pure joy, my brothers, whenever you face trials of various kinds, because you know that the testing of your faith produces perseverance." Moses's journey shows that adversity faced with faith and obedience is never wasted; it produces perseverance, wisdom, and a stronger trust in God's purpose. Our own challenges can become opportunities for growth if we allow God to shape our hearts.

The Power of Intercessory Prayer

Moses demonstrated the profound impact of intercessory prayer when he pleaded for the Israelites after their sin with the golden calf (Exodus 32). His prayers averted disaster and illustrated a leader's responsibility to intercede for others. This teaches us that:

- We are called to pray for those around us, even amid widespread failure.
- Intercession is an act of love and sacrifice, bearing others' burdens with empathy.
- God honors prayers rooted in genuine love and sorrow for sin.

As contemporary believers, Moses's example encourages us to develop fervent prayer habits, not only for ourselves but also for the restoration of our communities.

The Importance of Obedience

Obedience played a central role in the Israelites' journey. When they followed God's commands, they received His blessings and protection. Disobedience led to extended wandering and discipline, as seen in Moses's own experience at Meribah (Numbers 20). This narrative reminds us that while God is gracious, He expects faithful adherence to His Word. Obedience unlocks the fullness of God's promises, even when the journey is difficult.

Embracing Vulnerability

Moses's story is marked by vulnerability: from his initial reluctance to confront Pharaoh to his moments of anger and grief. His humanity shows that true leadership is not about being flawless but about embracing weaknesses. When we yield our inadequacies to God, His strength is revealed as growth and effective leadership.

Perseverance in Adversity

Leading the Israelites through the wilderness for forty years, Moses embodied perseverance. His unwavering commitment to God's call, despite setbacks, demonstrates that perseverance is an active, faith-driven pursuit rather than mere passive endurance. When our own journey seems impossible, Moses inspires us to keep moving forward, trusting that each step brings us closer to God's ultimate plan.

The Assurance of God's Presence

Perhaps the most comforting insight from the wilderness narrative is the reminder that God's presence accompanies us even in our darkest moments. Moses witnessed the pillar of cloud by day and the pillar of fire by night a perpetual sign that no matter how isolated or desperate we feel, God is there. This assurance is echoed in Joshua 1:9 (NKJV): Be strong and of good courage; do not be afraid, nor be dismayed, for the LORD your God is with you wherever you go. The personal insight here is profound: God's presence never fades. In our own trials, we can find hope knowing that each obstacle we face is never encountered alone.

The wilderness journey symbolizes trials that refine faith and leadership. Moses's guidance through divine provision, intercessory prayer, obedience, vulnerability, perseverance, and assurance of God's presence offers enduring lessons for overcoming adversity. Wilderness experiences highlight trust in God's continual guidance and the remarkable power of faith amid hardship.

Chapter 12- Lessons from the Ministry Builder

Integrating Moses's Experience into Contemporary Ministry

Modern ministers can draw directly from Moses's journey when developing a ministry. Moses was not a leader by self-proclamation but was chosen by God and performed mighty works ordained by Him. Today's ministry should similarly begin with a divine calling, a personal encounter with the living God, that imbues the leader with a sense of purpose and direction. The humility Moses exhibited in his reluctance can serve as a template for leaders to remain teachable and sensitive to God's leading, ensuring that pride does not overshadow the servant's heart necessary for genuine ministry.

Contemporary leaders should frequently remind themselves of their dependence on a higher authority. The NKJV scripture's repeated affirmation of God's presence, for example, "I will be with you" (Exodus 3:12), is a mantra that should guide modern ministry strategies. Leaders who ground their authority in God's promise find resilience in times of difficulty and are better equipped to handle successes and failures alike.

As epitomized by Moses, true authority is expressed through service. Leaders can emulate Moses by serving their communities, prioritizing their congregation's needs, and being accessible to those they lead. This servant leadership model encourages a culture of mutual respect and collective responsibility, where authority is not enforced but earned through empathy and genuine concern for others' welfare.

Moses often engaged in transparent dialogue with God and his people. His moments of intimation and vulnerability, for instance, his plea for intercession when Israel was angered, demonstrate that admitting one's limitations is a strength, not a weakness. Contemporary leadership practices would benefit greatly from similar accountability structures, where mentors, peers, and even the congregation hold the leader to high standards of honesty and service.

In Numbers 12, when Miriam and Aaron criticized Moses, God's response not only confirmed Moses's authority but also reminded him to guard against arrogance. Modern ministry must be open to constructive criticism. Recognizing that feedback is essential for growth ensures the leader does not become isolated in pride but remains open to learning and evolving. Over time, personal reflection upon Moses's story, especially through the NKJV's rich language, offers several revelatory insights that inform how ministry should be conducted today.

Moses's initial hesitance and self-doubt highlight a crucial truth: true ministry begins by acknowledging our own inadequacies. This vulnerability, when placed before God, can be transformed into courage through His promise of empowerment. The NKJV narrative shows that leadership in God's kingdom is counterintuitive to worldly expectations. Instead of accumulating power and prestige, ministers are called to sacrifice personal comfort for communal benefit. Moses's life is a study in balancing personal sacrifice with public responsibility.

A significant insight is the transformative partnership between the leader and the Divine. Moses's repeated encounters with God emphasize that authority is a shared responsibility between man and God, a lesson that reminds modern ministers to maintain a vibrant, ongoing relationship with the Lord through prayer, study, and obedience to the Word.

Moses's journey from call to commission is instructive. After his call in the burning bush, Moses was commissioned to deliver Israel. However, his ministry was marked by continuous learning, repeated reminders of God's promises, and perseverance despite setbacks. Contemporary ministry, too, should see the initial call not as a destination but as the beginning of a long journey of both personal and ministerial development.

Reflecting on Moses's struggles with the burdens of leadership, especially during times of national disobedience, reveals that ministry is never devoid of challenges. Yet, these challenges are opportunities for growth. The NKJV recounts Moses's prayer for mercy and his intercession on behalf of the nation, which continues to serve as a powerful reminder that leaders must carry the burdens of their people with both compassion and reliance on divine strength.

Implementing the Model

For modern ministries seeking to emulate Moses's example, several practical steps are worth considering. Like Moses, who was shaped by his early experiences in Egypt and Midian, contemporary leaders benefit from rigorous training grounded in Scripture, theology, and pastoral care. Seminars, workshops, and theological education can provide a strong doctrinal foundation while emphasizing the importance of humility and service.

A key element in Moses's life was his refinement through mentorship, whether through divine encounters or guidance from his father-in-law, Jethro (Exodus 18). Modern ministries should ensure that emerging leaders have seasoned mentors to help them discern God's voice and navigate the complexities of ministry with wisdom.

Establish systems of accountability that encourage leaders to share their struggles, receive feedback, and maintain transparency with peers and congregants.

These systems foster an environment where humility is prioritized, and authority is exercised responsibly.

Structuring ministry teams around the principle of servant leadership can transform how authority is perceived and exercised. In practice, this includes rotating leadership responsibilities, encouraging collaborative decision-making, and emphasizing community service as a core tenet of ministry.

Moses's ministry was deeply rooted in community-building among the Israelites. For contemporary ministries, building strong community ties is essential. Leaders should prioritize creating opportunities for service projects, outreach programs, and small groups that serve the congregation and reach out to the wider community. When authority is exercised with humility, communities are more willing to engage and collaborate.

Continuous regular Bible studies, prayer meetings, and spiritual retreats help reinforce a culture of humility and reliance on God. Just as Moses frequently returned to his lessons from the wilderness, modern ministries benefit from ongoing spiritual education and reflection. Just as Moses did not bear the entire burden of leadership alone, contemporary practice should emphasize teamwork, with authority shared among gifted individuals, ensuring that no single person becomes overburdened or distant from the people they serve.

While Moses's ministry occurred in a vastly different cultural and technological context, the underlying principles remain relevant. Today's ministers face unique challenges, including digital communication, cultural complexity, and global interconnectedness. However, these should not distract from the core biblical mandate of humility and divine authority. Ministers can leverage technology to reach broader audiences while always anchoring their message in timeless truths.

Use social media and online ministries in ways that mirror Moses's public proclamation of God's law. However, ensure that digital outreach remains personal and relational. In a diverse world, ministers must approach authority with cultural humility, understanding that while the gospel is universal, its expression may need to adapt to different cultural contexts without compromising core truths. As Moses was called to lead a nation, contemporary leaders can foster networks with ministries worldwide, encouraging a global perspective that transcends local or denominational boundaries.

Moses's hesitancy, contrasted with God's bold assertions of power, teaches that obedience even in the face of personal inadequacy is far more important than outward displays of confidence. True ministry is marked by a quiet trust in God, exemplified by Moses in his numerous encounters with the divine. Moses's history reveals that leadership is an evolving process. What begins as a divine call matures into an intricate interplay of decision-making, intercession, and accountability. This dynamic should serve as a reminder that one's ministry is never complete; it is a journey of continuous growth and reliance on God.

Here's another key for modern builders: Moses's deep connection with his people, even when he had to deliver tough judgments, underscores that empathy and compassion do not detract from authority; rather, they enrich it. Leaders who show genuine care for their congregation reflect the heart of Jesus, who himself modeled compassion and service. Perhaps the most profound insight is found in God's assurance in weakness. Moses's ability to lead despite personal shortcomings serves as a beacon of hope for any minister feeling inadequate. The NKJV repeatedly assures us that God's strength is made perfect in our weakness (see 2 Corinthians 12:9 NKJV), a principle Moses lived out every day.

The ministry of Moses offers timeless lessons in balancing humility with authority that are as relevant today as they were in ancient times. Moses's journey from his encounter at the burning bush to his role as the mediator of the covenant demonstrates that true leadership is not about personal glory but about a humble submission to God's call and a commitment to serving others.

In a world where authority is often equated with power and self-sufficiency, Moses's life reminds us that true authority flows out of humility, obedience, and a willingness to be shaped by God's presence. By anchoring our ministries in these timeless truths, we not only uphold the integrity of our calling but also make a lasting impact on the lives of those we lead and the ministries we build.

Chapter 13- The Moses Model

Leading Today with Moses's Model

Throughout Scripture, Moses stands as an iconic leader whose journey from reluctant shepherd to bold deliverer offers countless lessons for modern leadership. In a culture that often values power, control, and personal success, Moses's model is characterized by vulnerability, selfless accountability, and the delicate balance between humility and authority. Let him speak powerfully to leaders today.

Recall the central text in Exodus 3, where God appears to Moses in the burning bush. Moses is tending the flock of his father-in-law in Midian when he encounters God's holy presence; you know the story. In this passage, we observe Moses's initial reluctance and profound display of humility. God's assurance, "I will be with you" (Exodus 3:12 NKJV), underscores a critical principle: true leadership is founded on divine partnership rather than personal prowess.

This interaction sets the stage for Moses's entire ministry. His leadership is not self-generated; rather, it is activated by God's command. Modern leaders can learn that stepping into a leadership role may often feel overwhelming, yet the assurance of divine support can transform perceived weakness into strength. Moses's model reminds us that even in moments of self-doubt, reliance on God can enable us to carry out extraordinary tasks.

Let's examine the first key: vulnerability. Moses's reluctance at the burning bush is one of many examples of this trait, inviting his audience to understand that true authority in God's service is not self-propelled but God-ordained. When Moses was first confronted with God's call, his honesty before God served as an example of idea vulnerability: I am not eloquent, either in the past or since you have spoken to your servant" (Exodus 4:10 NKJV).

This candid admission of his own limitations is profoundly important to today's leaders, who are often expected to be flawless. Moses's acknowledgment that he is less than perfect, yet still chosen by God, illustrates that vulnerability can be a source of strength. It allows a leader to build deeper connections with others and fosters a culture of authenticity and humility.

118

The next key of the Moses model is selfless accountability. Moses repeatedly placed the needs of the Israelites above his personal concerns. When the people rebelled, criticized his leadership, or even questioned God's provision, Moses interceded on their behalf. In Numbers 14, when the people murmured against God after hearing of the imminent challenges in the Promised Land, Moses assumed the burden of their sin, pleading for God's mercy even while his own heart was heavy with their discontent.

This intercessory role demonstrates how accountability and selflessness define true leadership. Today's leaders can learn from Moses by prioritizing the welfare of those they lead, listening to their struggles, addressing their needs, and interceding on their behalf when necessary. In a time when leadership can often be impersonal or self-serving, Moses's manner of service is both refreshing and instructive.

One of the hallmarks of Moses's leadership model is his ability to balance godly authority with deep humility. Although he was chosen to deliver an entire nation from bondage, Moses continually recognized that his authority came from God's hand. Moses's signs and wonders, the turning of his staff to a serpent, the transformation of his hand, and the eventual parting of the Red Sea were not his own doing but miraculous confirmations of God's power (Exodus 4:2-4 NKJV). These acts affirmed that his leadership was an extension of divine authority. This reality teaches modern leaders that their influence and success should be credited to a power greater than themselves. When leaders acknowledge that their abilities come from God, they guard against both pride and autocracy, remaining humble stewards of the gifts given to them.

Applying Moses's Model to Contemporary Leadership

The principles derived from Moses's leadership are not confined to ancient history; they provide practical guidelines for navigating the complexities of today's ministry, corporate environments, and community leadership structures. In an era where leaders are expected to have all the answers, Moses's example teaches us that a call to leadership often exceeds our personal capacities. Modern leaders face great challenges from economic turmoil to social divisions, but like Moses, they can trust that their effectiveness lies in a partnership with a higher power. Leaders who ground their decisions in prayer, meditation on Scripture, and sustained worship are better equipped to overcome personal shortcomings, thus allowing God's strength to work through their vulnerabilities.

Moses did not work in isolation. Over the years, he learned the importance of delegating responsibilities and relying on trusted advisors. In Exodus 18, Jethro's advice to Moses is a powerful lesson: You shall now provide for the people, according to their numbers, every man his work...(Exodus 18:21 NKJV). In today's leadership landscape, whether in church ministry, business, or non-profit organizations, creating strong teams built on mutual respect, accountability, and the willingness to serve one another can prevent burnout and enhance overall effectiveness. Leaders should foster environments where each team member feels valued and where hierarchical boundaries are softened by the understanding that ultimate authority rests in a commitment to serve the common good.

Moses's leadership was characterized by ongoing dialogue with God and his people. His willingness to admit mistakes (as seen in moments of frustration and self-doubt) shows that accountability is not a weakness but a critical aspect of healthy leadership. Modern leaders can take inspiration from Moses by establishing systems of accountability within their organizations. Whether through mentorship, peer review, or open discussion forums, creating spaces where honest feedback is welcome can help sustain the leader's humility and ensure that authority is exercised responsibly.

Perhaps one of the most enduring lessons from Moses's life is his role as a crisis leader. During the plagues in Egypt, the parting of the Red Sea, and the challenges of the wilderness, Moses was constantly reminded that his leadership was not immune to crises. Instead of conceding to despair, he leaned into his divine mandate. Modern leaders, especially in times of uncertainty, whether due to public health crises, economic instability, or societal unrest, can find comfort in knowing that God's promise, I will be with you (Exodus 3:12 NKJV), transcends every difficulty. This faith fosters resilience and instills courage, enabling leaders to guide their communities through turbulent circumstances.

Reflecting on Moses's model through the lens of NKJV scripture yields personal revelations that resonate on both spiritual and practical levels. Moses's repeated expressions of inadequacy, "Who am I…" and "I am not eloquent," serve as continual reminders that leadership is not judged merely by outward competence or charisma but by the heart and integrity behind every decision. In my own experiences, I have found that acknowledging my limitations has opened the door to receiving advice, wisdom, and support from colleagues and mentors. The humility Moses displayed encourages me to remain grounded, for it is in the space of humility that true service to others flourishes.

Every modern challenge seems to bring with it a chorus of competing voices and pressures; yet, the assurance Moses found in God's promise "I will be with you" has become a personal touchstone. When confronted with daunting decisions or moments of self-doubt, recalling that reliance on divine strength can transform weakness into power has been transformative. This insight has not only shaped my professional journey but also deepened my spiritual walk. It reminds me that effective leadership is not about self-sufficiency but about leaning on the everlasting strength provided by God's faithful presence.

Moses's journey was not one of overnight success; it was a gradual process of refinement through hardship. His leadership in the face of rebellion, frustration, and the ever-present weight of responsibility continues to challenge contemporary leaders to persevere even when the road seems unending. This perspective is particularly resonant in today's fast-paced world, where immediate results are often expected. Moses's example teaches that perseverance, marked by consistent effort and faith, ultimately yields growth and success that are both lasting and life-changing.

Leading today with Moses's model is not simply about adopting an ancient style of leadership; it is about embracing the timeless principles that Moses exemplified: humility, obedience, servant leadership, and unwavering trust in God. His story, as preserved in the NKJV scriptures, teaches us that effective leadership is less about projecting authority and more about inviting divine empowerment into every decision. In every chapter of Moses's journey from the burning bush to the parting of the Red Sea, there is a reminder that leadership is both a sacred calling and a profound act of service.

By embracing these timeless principles, modern leaders can not only navigate today's complexities but also leave an indelible mark on their communities, echoing Moses's legacy of a leadership that transforms challenges into channels for God's grace and love.

Conclusion

As I conclude these reflections on leading today with Moses's model, I am reminded that leadership is a divine appointment, one that calls us to step beyond our limitations and into a place of service where authority is balanced by humility. In a world that often confuses power with dominance, Moses stands as a beacon who redefines leadership as an act of obedience, trust, and lasting commitment to the well-being of others. May each leader inspired by Moses find solace and strength in the eternal promise of God's presence, and may our collective efforts strive to serve with grace and genuine compassion.

This comprehensive reflection on ancient leadership for modern times serves not only as an exposition of biblical truth but also as a personal invitation to re-examine our own roles as leaders. Let Moses's life be a continual reminder that great leadership does not depend on human ability alone, but on a humble heart that trusts, listens, and perseveres under divine guidance.

About the Author

Dwayne is married to Esther Marcellus-Perry. He is a dedicated servant of Christ and passionate about empowering individuals to reach their full potential. With a heart rooted in love and a deep desire to see others thrive, he serves others out of an apostolic anointing. Driven by a genuine love for people, Dwayne seeks to uplift and inspire through coaching, mentoring, writing, teaching, and ministry.

Dwayne is a remarkable individual who has attained his Doctorate in Education and Ministry. His life's journey has been marked by excellence, service, education, and a deep commitment to empowering others. With a 13-year career as a professional basketball player, Dwayne's passion for sports and unwavering dedication to his craft have shaped who he is today. Beyond his achievements on the court, Dwayne's true calling lies in his ability to serve others out of an apostolic anointing. Recognized as an anointed teacher, he possesses a unique gift for imparting wisdom and inspiring transformation in the lives of those he encounters. Through his teachings, Dwayne has touched countless hearts, helping individuals unlock their full potential and discover their purpose.

As a coach, mentor, and developer of people, he has made it his mission to guide others on their journey toward personal and professional growth.

His commitment to nurturing talent and fostering a spirit of excellence has earned him the respect and admiration of those he has had the privilege to work with. Dwayne's ability to see the potential in others and empower them to reach new heights is a testament to his servant-hearted nature.

In addition to his athletic and teaching prowess, Dwayne is a sought-after speaker and motivator. His captivating presence and ability to connect with diverse audiences make him a powerful force for change. Through his engaging talks, he challenges individuals to overcome obstacles, embrace their unique gifts, and live a life of purpose and significance. His life experiences, both on and off the court, have shaped his character and fueled his passion for making a positive impact. His unwavering commitment to serving others, combined with his natural leadership abilities, has positioned him as a catalyst for transformation in the lives of many.

As you embark on this journey through the pages of this book, allow Dwayne's wisdom, insights, and experiences to inspire and empower you. His unique blend of athletic prowess, spiritual anointing, and dedication to developing people will undoubtedly leave a lasting impact on your life. Prepare to be challenged, motivated, and equipped as you delve into the transformative teachings of Dr. Dwayne C. Perry, a former professional basketball player, an anointed teacher, a coach, mentor, and a developer of people.